AA Essential

German
phrase book

AA Publishing

Contents

English edition prepared by First Edition Translations Ltd, Great Britain

Designed and produced by AA Publishing

Distributed in the United Kingdom by AA Publishing, Norfolk House,
Priestley Road, Basingstoke, Hampshire RG24 9NY

First published in 1993 as Wat & Hoe Duits, © Uitgeverij Kosmos bv -
Utrecht/Antwerpen

Van Dale Lexicografie bv - Utrecht/Antwerpen

This edition © The Automobile Association 1997

Reprinted 1997
Reprinted Mar and Sep 1998

A CIP catalogue record for this book is available from the
British Library

ISBN: 0 7495 1472 8

Published by AA Publishing (a trading name of Automobile Association
Developments Limited, whose registered office is Norfolk House,
Priestley Road, Basingstoke, Hampshire RG24 9NY.
Registered number 1878835).

Typeset by Anton Graphics Ltd, Andover, Hampshire

Printed & bound by G. Canale C.spa, Torino Italy

Cover photographs: Museum fur Verkehr und Technick, Berlin, AA
Photo Library (A. Souter); Oktoberfest, Munich, Pictor International -
London; Charlottenburg Palace, Berlin, AA Photo Library (A. Baker)

Find out more about AA Publishing and the wide range of services the
AA provides by visiting our web site at www.theaa.co.uk

Introduction

● **Welcome to the AA's new Essential Phrase Books series, covering the most popular European languages and containing everything you'd expect from a comprehensive language series. They're concise, accessible and easy to understand, and you'll find them indispensable on your trip abroad.**

Each guide is divided into 15 themed sections and starts with a pronunciation table which explains the phonetic pronunciation to all the words and phrases you'll need to know for your trip, while at the back of the book is an extensive word list and grammar guide which will help you construct basic sentences in your chosen language.

Throughout the book you'll come across coloured boxes with a 🕲 beside them. These are designed to help you if you can't understand what your listener is saying to you. Hand the book over to them and encourage them to point to the appropriate answer to the question you are asking.

Other coloured boxes in the book - this time without the symbol - give alphabetical listings of themed words with their English translations beside them.

For extra clarity, we have put all English words and phrases in black, foreign language terms in red and their phonetic pronunciation in italic.

This phrase book covers all subjects you are likely to come across during the course of your visit, from reserving a room for the night to ordering food and drink at a restaurant and what to do if your car breaks down or you lose your traveller's cheques and money. With over 2,000 commonly used words and essential phrases at your fingertips you can rest assured that you will be able to get by in all situations, so let the Essential Phrase Book become your passport to a secure and enjoyable trip!

Pronunciation guide

The pronunciation provided should be read as if it were English,
bearing in mind the following main points:

Vowels

a	is like **ar**	ar	as in **Kater**	karter
	or the **u** in cup	u	as in **Tasse**	tusser
ä	is like **ay** in may	ay	as in **spät**	shpayt
	or **e** in edible	e	as in **hält**	helt
e	is like **ay** in may	ay	as in **Nebel**	naybel
	or **e** in edible	e	as in **Mensch**	mensh
	or **air** in fair	air	as in **Schmerz**	shmairts
i	is like **i** in lick	i	as in **Mitte**	mitter
o	is like **oa** in boat	oa	as in **Motor**	moator
	or **o** in lock	o	as in **Socke**	zokker
ö	is like **u** in fur	oe	as in **öffnen**	oefnen
u	is like **oo** in ooze	oo	as in **Kur**	koor
ü	is like **ue** in cue	ue	as in **fünf**	fuenf

Consonants

Consonants are mainly as in English except for

g	like **g** in great	g	as in **Gigant**	gigant
j	like **y** in yes	y	as in **ja**	yar
s	when at beginning of word, like **z**	z	as in **Seife**	zaifer
v	like **f** in fish	f	as in **Volk**	folk
w	like **v** in vole	v	as in **Wagen**	vargen
z	like **ts** in cats	ts	as in **zwölf**	tsvoelf

At the end of a word **b**, **d**, and **g** change in sound to **p**, **t** and **k**
respectively. The symbol **ß** (es-tset) stands for **ss** and is rare.

Some combinations of letters

au is pronounced *ow* as in cow; **eu** and **äu** are pronounced *oy* as in boy;
ie is pronounced *ee* as in feet; **ei** and **ai** are pronounced as *ai* in Thai; **ch**
is like **ch** in loch but rendered in the pronunciation as *kh*; **qu** is
pronounced *kv*; **sp** and **st** at the start of a word are pronounced *shp* and
sht; **sch** is also pronounced *sh*.

Stress

Usually on the leading syllable or on the stem (root) of the word, e.g.
stehen (to stand) is stressed *shtayen*, **verstehen** (to understand) is
stressed fair*shtayen*.

Useful lists

1 Useful lists

1.1 Today or tomorrow?

What day is it today? _____	Welcher Tag ist heute? *velkher tark ist hoyter?*
Today's Monday_____	Heute ist Montag *hoyter ist moantark*
– Tuesday_____	Heute ist Dienstag *hoyter ist deenstark*
– Wednesday _____	Heute ist Mittwoch *hoyter ist mittvokh*
– Thursday_____	Heute ist Donnerstag *hoyter ist donnerstark*
– Friday_____	Heute ist Freitag *hoyter ist fraitark*
– Saturday _____	Heute ist Samstag/Sonnabend (S. Germany/ N. Germany) *hoyter ist zamstark/zonnarbent*
– Sunday _____	Heute ist Sonntag *hoyter ist zonntark*
in January _____	im Januar *im yannooar*
since February _____	seit Februar *zait febrooar*
in spring_____	im Frühling *im fruehling*
in summer _____	im Sommer *im zommer*
in autumn _____	im Herbst *im hairpst*
in winter_____	im Winter *im vinter*
1997_____	neunzehnhundertsiebenundneunzig *noyntsayn hoondert zeeben oont noyntsikh*
the twentieth century _____	das zwanzigste Jahrhundert *dass tsvantsikhster yarhoondert*
What's the date today? ____	Der wievielte ist heute? *dayr veefeelter ist hoyter?*
Today's the 24th_____	Heute ist der vierundzwanzigste *hoyter ist dayr fear oont tsvantsikhster*
Monday 3 November 1998	Montag, der 3 November 1998 *moantark dayr dritter november noyntsayn hoondert akht oont noyntsikh*
in the morning _____	morgens *morgens*
midday _____	mittags (from about 11.30 - 2.00 p.m.) *mittarks*
in the afternoon _____	nachmittags *nakhmittarks*
in the evening _____	abends *arbents*
at night_____	nachts *nakhts*
this morning_____	heute morgen *hoyter morgen*

this afternoon _____	heute mittag
	hoyter mittark
this evening _____	heute nachmittag
	hoyter nakhmittark
tonight _____	heute abend
	hoyter arbent
last night _____	letzte nacht
	letster nakht
this week _____	diese Woche
	deezer vokher
next month _____	nächsten Monat
	nexten moanart
last year _____	voriges Jahr
	forigez yar
next... _____	nächste(n)/nächstes...
	nexter(n)/nextes
in...days/weeks/ _____	in ... Tagen/Wochen/Monaten/Jahren
months/years	*in ... targen/vokhen/moanarten/yaren*
...weeks ago _____	vor ... Wochen
	for ... vokhen
day off _____	der freie Tag
	dayr fraier tark

 .2 Bank holidays

● **The most important** bank holidays in Germany are the following:

January 1	New Year's Day (Neujahr)
January 6	Epiphany (Hl. Drei Könige)
March/April	Good Friday, Easter and Easter Monday (Karfreitag, Ostersonntag und Ostermontag
May 1	May Day (Maifeiertag)
May	Ascension Day (Christi Himmelfahrt)
May/June	Whit Sunday and Whit Monday (Pfingstsonntag und Pfingstmontag)
*June	Corpus Christi (Fronleichnam)
*August 15	Feast of the Assumption (Mariä Himmelfahrt)
October 3	Day of German Unity (Tag der deutschen Einheit)
*November 1	All Saint's Day (Allerheiligen)
*November (Wed, variable)	Buss- und Bettag (day to repent and pray)
December 25/26	Christmas (Weihnachten)

Most shops, banks and government institutions are closed on these days. The dates marked with an asterisk are Catholic holidays and are mainly celebrated in the south of Germany. On Christmas Eve banks and shops tend to be closed in the afternoon.

Useful lists

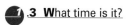

.3 What time is it?

What time is it? _____	Wie spät ist es?
	vee shpayt ist ez?
It's nine o'clock _____	Es ist neun Uhr
	ez ist noyn ooer
– five past ten _____	Es ist fünf nach zehn
	ez ist fuenf nakh tsayn
– a quarter past eleven ___	Es ist Viertel nach elf
	ez ist feartel nakh elf
– twenty past twelve_____	Es ist zehn nach zwölf
	ez ist tsayn nakh tsvoelf
– half past one _____	Es ist halb zwei
	ez ist halp tsvai
– twenty–five to three_____	Es ist fünf nach halb drei
	ez ist fuenf nakh halp drai
– a quarter to four_____	Es ist Viertel vor vier
	ez ist feartel for fear
– ten to five _____	Es ist zehn vor fünf
	ez ist tsayn for fuenf
– twelve noon_____	Es ist zwölf
	ez ist tsvoelf
– midnight _____	Es ist Mitternacht
	ez ist mitternakht
half an hour _____	eine halbe Stunde
	ainer halber shtoonder
What time? _____	Um wieviel Uhr?
	oom veefeel ooer?
What time can I come ____ round?	Wann kann ich vorbeikommen?
	vann kann ikh for bai kommen?
At... _____	Um...*oom...*
After... _____	Nach...*nakh...*
Before... _____	Vor...*for...*
Between...and... _____	Zwischen... und...
	tsvishen ... oont...
From...to... _____	Von ... bis...
	fon ... biss...
In...minutes _____	In ... Minuten
	in ... meenooten
– an hour _____	In einer Stunde
	in ainer shtoonder
– ...hours _____	In... Stunden
	In... shtoonden
– a quarter of an hour ____	In einer Viertelstunde
	in ainer feartel shtoonder
– three quarters of_____ an hour	In einer Dreiviertelstunde
	in ainer drai feartel shtoonder
early/late _____	zu früh/spät
	tsoo frue/shpayt
on time_____	rechtzeitig
	rekht tsaitikh
summertime _____	(die) Sommerzeit
	(dee) zommer tsait
wintertime_____	(die) Winterzeit
	(dee) vinter tsait

0	null	*nooll*
1	eins	*ains*
2	zwei	*tsvai*
3	drei	*drai*
4	vier	*fear*
5	fünf	*fuenf*
6	sechs	*zekhs*
7	sieben	*zeeben*
8	acht	*akht*
9	neun	*noyn*
10	zehn	*tsayn*
11	elf	*elf*
12	zwölf	*tsvoelf*
13	dreizehn	*draitsayn*
14	vierzehn	*feartsayn*
15	fünfzehn	*fuenftsayn*
16	sechzehn	*zekhtsayn*
17	siebzehn	*zeeptsayn*
18	achtzehn	*akht-tsayn*
19	neunzehn	*noyntsayn*
20	zwanzig	*tsvantsik*
21	einundzwanzig	*ain oont tsvantsik*
22	zweiundzwanzig	*tsvai oont tsvantsik*
30	dreissig	*draissik*
31	einunddreissig	*ain oont draissik*
32	zweiunddreissig	*tsvai oont draissik*
40	vierzig	*feartsik*
50	fünfzig	*fuenftsik*
60	sechzig	*zekhtsik*
70	siebzig	*zeeptsik*
80	achtzig	*akhttsik*
90	neunzig	*noyntsik*
100	hundert	*hoondert*
101	hunderteins	*hoondert ains*
110	hundertzehn	*hoondert tsayn*
120	hundertzwanzig	*hoondert tsvantsik*
200	zweihundert	*tsvai hoondert*
300	dreihundert	*drai hoondert*
400	vierhundert	*fear hoondert*
500	fünfhundert	*fuenf hoondert*
600	sechshundert	*zekhs hoondert*
700	siebenhundert	*zeeben hoondert*
800	achthundert	*akht hoondert*
900	neunhundert	*noyn hoondert*
1,000	tausend	*towzent*
1,100	tausendeinhundert	*towzent ain hoondert*
2,000	zweitausend	*tsvai towzent*
10,000	zehntausend	*tsayn towzent*
100,000	hunderttausend	*hoondert towzent*
1,000,000	eine Million	*ainer millioan*

1st _____	erste *erster*
2nd _____	zweite *tsvaiter*
3rd _____	dritte *dritter*
4th _____	vierte *fearter*
5th _____	fünfte *fuenfter*
6th _____	sechste *zekhster*
7th _____	sieb(en)te *zeeb(en)ter*
8th _____	achte *akhter*
9th _____	neunte *noynter*
10th _____	zehnte *tsaynter*
11th _____	elfte *elfter*
12th _____	zwölfte *tsvoelfter*
13th _____	dreizehnter *draitsaynter*
14th _____	vierzehnte *feartsaynter*
15th _____	fünfzehnte *fuenftsaynter*
16th _____	sechzehnte *zekhtsaynter*
17th _____	siebzehnte *zeeptsaynter*
18th _____	achtzehnte *akht-tsaynter*
19th _____	neunzehnte *noyntsaynter*
20th _____	zwanzigste *tsvantsikhster*
21st _____	einundzwanzigste *ain oont tsvantsikhster*
22nd _____	zweiundzwanzigste *tsvai oont tsvantsikhster*
30th _____	dreissigste *draissikhster*
100th _____	hundertste *hoondertster*
1,000th _____	tausendste *towzentster*
once _____	einmal *ainmarl*
twice _____	zweimal *tsvaimarl*
double _____	das Doppelte *dass doppelter*
triple _____	das Dreifache *dass draifakher*
half _____	die Hälfte *dee haelfter*
a quarter _____	ein Viertel *ain feartel*
a third _____	ein Drittel *ain dritel*
a couple, a few, some _____	ein paar, einige, mehrere *ain par, ainiger, mayrerer*
2+4=6 _____	zwei und vier ist sechs *tsvai oont fear ist zekhs*
4-2=2 _____	vier weniger zwei ist zwei *fear vayniger tsvai ist tsvai*
2x4=8 _____	zwei mal vier ist acht *tsvai marl fear ist akht*
4÷2=2 _____	vier geteilt durch zwei ist zwei *fear getailt doorkh tsvai ist tsvai*
odd/even _____	gerade/ungerarde *gerarder/oongerader*
total _____	(ins)gesamt *(ins)gezammt*
6x9 _____	sechs mal neun *zekhs marl noyn*

12

Is the weather going to be good/bad?	Wird das Wetter schön/schlecht?	_virt dass vetter shoen/shlekht?_
Is it going to get colder/hotter?	Wird es kälter/wärmer?	_virt es kaelter/vaermer?_
What temperature is it going to be?	Wieviel Grad wird es?	_veefeel grart virt ez?_
Is it going to rain?	Wird es regnen?	_virt ez raygnen?_
Is there going to be a storm?	Bekommen wir Sturm?	_bekommen veer shturm?_
Is it going to snow?	Wird es schneien?	_virt es shnaien?_
Is it going to freeze?	Wird es frieren?	_virt es freeren?_
Is the thaw setting in?	Wird es tauen?	_virt es towen?_
Is it going to be foggy?	Bekommen wir Nebel?	_bekommen veer naybel?_
Is there going to be a thunderstorm?	Wird es ein Gewitter geben?	_virt es ain gevitter gayben?_
The weather's changing	Das Wetter schlägt um	_dass vetter shlaekt oom_
It's cooling down	Es kühlt sich ab	_ez kuehlt zikh ap_
What's the weather going to be like today	Was für Wetter wird heute?	_vass fuer vetter virt hoyter?_

Bewölkung cloud	kalt cold	Rückenwind tail wind
Böen squalls	klar clear	Schnee snow
frisch chilly (temperature), fresh (wind)	kühl chilly	schwül muggy
	leicht bewölkt cloudy	sehr heiss scorching hot
Frost frost	leichte Bewölkung light clouds	sonnig sunny
Glatteis black ice	mild mild	Sprühregen drizzle
... Grad (unter/über Null) ... degrees (above/below zero)	nasskalt cold and damp	stark bewölkt overcast
	Nebel fog	starke Bewölkung heavy clouds
Graupel/Hagel hail	Orkan hurricane	Sturm storm
heiter fine	rauh bleak	Wind (leichter/ mässiger/starker) light/moderate/strong wind
heiss hot	Regenschauer shower	
Hitzewelle heat wave	Regen(schauer) rain	windig windy

See also 5.1 Asking for directions

Useful lists

here/there	hier/da
	heer/dar
somewhere/nowhere	irgendwo/nirgendwo
	eergentvoa/neergentvoa
everywhere	überall
	ueberall
far away/nearby	weit weg/inder Nähe
	vait vek/in dayr nayher
right/left	nach rechts/links
	nakh rekhts/links
to the right/left of	rechts/links von
	rekhts/links fon
straight ahead	geradeaus
	gerarder ows
via	über
	ueber
in	in
	in
on	auf
	owf
under	unter
	oonter
against	gegen
	gaygen
opposite	gegenüber
	gaygen ueber
next to	neben
	nayben
near	bei
	bai
in front of	vor
	for
in the centre	in der Mitte
	in dayr mitter
forward	nach vorn
	nakh forn
down	(nach) unten
	(nakh) oonten
up	(nach) oben
	(nakh) owben
inside	drinnen
	drinnen
outside	draussen/raus
	drowssen/rows
behind	(nach) hinten
	(nakh) hinten
at the front	vorn
	forn
at the back	hinten
	hinten
in the north	im Norden
	im norden

to the south_____	nach Süden	
	nakh zueden	
from the west_____	aus dem Westen	
	ows dem vesten	
from the east _____	aus dem Osten	
	ows daym ossten	
north, east, _____	nördlich/östlich/südlich/westlich von	
south, west of	*noerdlikh/oestlikh/zuedlikh/vestlikh fon*	

.7 What does that sign say?

See 5.4 Traffic signs

Abfahrt	Fussgänger	Rundfahrt
exit	pedestrians	tour
Achtung	Gasthaus/Gasthof	Schliessfach
beware	inn	left luggage
Ankunft	Gefahr	locker/safe deposit
arrival	danger	box
Aufzug	Geöffnet	Schwimmbad
lift	open	swimming-pool
Ausgang	Gepäckannahme/	Selbstbedienung
exit	-aufbewahrung	self-service
Auskunft	check-in/left-luggage	Stock
information	Geschlossen	floor
Bahnhof	closed	Treppe
station	Gleis	stairs
Bitte nicht stören	platform	Vorsicht!
Do not disturb	Hausmeister	beware
Drücken	caretaker	Warnung
push	Herein!	beware/warning
Durchgang	Come in!	Warteraum/-saal
throughway	Kein Trinkwasser	waiting room
Eingang	No drinking water	Wechselstube
entrance	Nicht berühren!	exchange office
Eintritt frei/verboten	Please do not touch!	Ziehen
free entry/no entry	Notausgang/-treppe	pull
Empfang	emergency	Zimmer frei/zu
reception	exit/stairs	vermieten
Erste Hilfe	Öffnungszeiten	vacancy (room)/
first aid	opening hours	room to let
Fahrkarten	Pförtner	Zugang
tickets	porter	access/entry
Fahrstuhl	Polizei	
lift	police	
Freibad	Rathaus	
open-air swimming-	town hall/city hall	
pool	Rauchen verboten	
Fremdenverkehrs-	no smoking	
verein	Reserviert	
tourist information	reserved	

15

.8 Telephone alphabet

a	ar	wie Anton	vee arnton
ä	ay	wie Ärger	vee airger
b	beh	wie Berta	vee berter
c	tseh	wie Cäsar	vee tsezer
ch	tseh-har	wie Charlotte	vee sharlotter
d	deh	wie Dora	vee doara
e	eh	wie Emil	vee aymil
f	ef	wie Friedrich	vee freedrikh
g	geh	wie Gustav	vee goostaf
h	hah	wie Heinrich	vee hainrikh
i	ee	wie Ida	vee eeda
j	yot	wie Julius	vee yoolius
k	kah	wie Kaufmann	vee kowfmann
l	el	wie Ludwig	vee loodvikh
m	em	wie Martha	vee marta
n	en	wie Nordpol	vee nortpole
o	oh	wie Otto	vee ottoa
ö	oe	wie Ökonom	vee oekonoam
p	peh	wie Paula	vee powla
q	koo	wie Quelle	vee kveller
r	air	wie Richard	vee rikhart
sch	es-tseh-har	wie Schule	vee shooler
s	es	wie Samuel	vee zarmooel
t	teh	wie Theodor	vee tayoador
u	oo	wie Ulrich	vee oolrikh
ü	ue	wie Übermut	vee uebermoot
v	fow	wie Viktor	vee viktor
w	veh	wie Wilhelm	vee vilhelm
x	iks	wie Xanthippe	vee ksantippeh
y	uepsilon	wie Ypsilon	vee uepsilon
z	tset	wie Zacharias	vee tsakharias

.9 Personal details

surname	(der) Nachname	
	(dayr) nakhnarmer	
christian name	(der) Vorname	
	(dayr) fornarmer	
initials	(der) Anfangsbuchstabe des Vornamens	
	(dayr) an-fangs-bookh-shtarber dess fornarmenz	
address (street/ number)	(die) Anschrift (Strasse/Nummer)	
	(dee) anshrift (shtrasser/noommer)	
post code/town	(die) Postleitzahl/(der) Wohnort	
	(dee) posst-lait-tsarl/(dayr) voanort	
sex (male/female)	(das) Geschlecht (m.= männlich, w.= weiblich)	
	(dass) geschlekht (m.= maennlikh, w. = vaiblikh)	
nationality	(die) Staatsangehörigkeit	
	(dee) shtarts-ange-hoerikh-kait	
date of birth	(das) Geburtsdatum	
	(dass) geboorts dartum	

place of birth _____	(der) Geburtsort
	(dayr) geboorts ort
occupation _____	(der) Beruf
	(dayr) beroof
married/single/ _____ divorced	verheiratet/ledig/geschieden
	fairhai-rartet/laydikh/gescheeden
widowed _____	(die) Witwe/(der) Witwer
	(dee) vitveh/ (dayr) vitver
(number of) children _____	(Zahl der) Kinder
	(tsarl dayr) kinder
identity card/passport/ _____ driving licence number	Personalausweis/Reisepass/Führerschein-nummer,
	pair zoanarl owsvaiz-raizerparss/fuerershain-nummer
place and date of issue _____	Ort und Datum der Ausstellung
	ort oont dartoom dayr owsshtelloong

Courtesies

2 Courtesies

● **It is usual in Germany** to shake hands on meeting and parting company.

2 .1 Greetings

● **The correct pronoun** to use in formal greetings is '*Sie*' (zee) - which translates as 'you' - in the singular and plural. '*Sie*' should be employed when addressing people over the age of 18 except when talking to intimates. Conversation within the family, or between children, youths, students, friends and close work colleagues requires the use of the familiar second person pronoun '*du*' (doo). Please note that amongst adults it is usual for the older person to offer the more familiar address of '*du*' to the younger one.

Hello, Mr... _____	Guten Tag, Herr...
	gooten tark, hair...
Hello, Mrs... _____	Guten Tag, Frau...
	gooten tark, frow...
Hello, Peter _____	Hallo, Peter
	hallo, payter
Hi, Helen _____	Tag, Helene
	tark, helayner
Good morning _____	Guten Morgen
	gooten morgen
Good afternoon _____	Guten Tag
	gooten tark
Good evening_____	Guten Abend
	gooten arbent
How are you? _____	Wie geht's?
	vee gayts?
Fine, thank you, and you?__	Sehr gut, und Ihnen?
	zayr goot, oont eenen?
Very well _____	Ausgezeichnet
	ows ge tsaikh net
Not very well _____	Nicht besonders
	nikht bezonderz
Not too bad_____	Es geht
	ez gayt
I'd better be going_____	Dann geh' ich mal
	dann gay' ikh mall
I have to be going. _____	Ich muss los. Ich werde erwartet
Someone's waiting for me	*ikh mooss loas. ikh verder ervartet*
Bye!_____	Tschüs
	tshuess
Goodbye _____	Auf Wiedersehen
	owf veederzayn
See you soon _____	Bis bald
	biss balt
See you later _____	Bis gleich
	biss glaich
See you in a little while____	Bis dann
	biss dann
Sleep well _____	Schlafen Sie gut
	shlarfen zee goot

Good night	Gute Nacht
	gooter nakht
All the best	Alles Gute
	alles gooter
Have fun	Viel Vergnügen
	feel fairgnuegen
Good luck	Viel Glück
	feel gluek
Have a nice holiday	(Einen) schönen Urlaub
	(ainen) shoenen oorlowp
Have a good trip	Gute Reise
	gooter raizer
Thank you, you too	Danke, gleichfalls
	danker, glaikhfalz
Say hello to...for me	Schöne Grüsse an...
	shoener gruesser an...

.2 How to ask a question

Who?	Wer?
	vayr?
Who's that?	Wer ist das?
	vayr ist dass?
What?	Was?
	vass?
What's there to see here?	Was gibt es hier zu sehen?
	vass gipt ez heer tsoo zayhen?
What kind of hotel is that?	Was für eine Art Hotel ist das?
	vass fuer ainer art hotel ist dass?
Where?	Wo?
	voe?
Where's the toilet?	Wo ist die Toilette?
	voe ist dee twaletter?
Where are you going?	Wohin gehen/(by car) fahren Sie?
	vohin gayhen/fahren zee?
Where are you from?	Woher kommen Sie?
	vohair kommen zee?
How?	Wie?
	vee?
How far is that?	Wie weit ist das?
	vee vait ist dass?
How long does that take?	Wie lange dauert das?
	vee langer dowert dass?
How long is the trip?	Wie lange dauert die Reise?
	vee langer dowert dee raizer?
How much?	Wieviel?
	veefeel?
How much is this?	Wieviel kostet das?
	veefeel kostet dass?
What time is it?	Wie spät ist es?
	vee shpayt ist ez?
Which?	Welcher (masculine), welches (neuter), welche (feminine, plural)
	velkher? velkherz? velkher?
Which glass is mine?	Welches Glas ist für mich?
	velkherz glars ist fuer mikh?

English	German
When? _____	Wann? *vann?*
When are you leaving? ___	Wann reisen Sie ab? *vann raizen zee ap?*
Why? _____	Warum? *vahroom?*
Could you...me? _____	Können Sie mir/mich... *koennen zee meer/mikh...*
Could you help me, please?	Könnten Sie mir bitte helfen? *koennten zee meer bitter helfen?*
Could you point that out to me?	Können Sie mir das zeigen? *koennen zee meer dass tsaygen?*
Could you come with me, please?	Würden Sie bitte mit mir mitgehen? *vuerden zee bitter mit meer mitgayhen?*
Could you... _____	Würden Sie bitte...? *vuerden zee bitter...?*
Could you reserve some tickets for me, please?	Würden Sie bitte Karten für mich reservieren? *vuerden zee bitter karten fuer mikh rezerveeren?*
Do you know...?	Wissen Sie...? *vissen zee...?*
Do you know another hotel, please?	Könnten Sie mir ein anderes Hotel empfehlen? *koennten zee meer ain anderez hotel empfaylen?*
Do you know whether...? ___	Wissen Sie ob.. *vissen zee op...*
Do you have a...? _____	Haben Sie ein(en)/eine...? *harben zee ain(en)/ainer...?*
Do you have a vegetarian dish, please?	Haben Sie bitte ein vegetarisches Gericht? *harben zee bitter ain vegetarishers gerikht?*
I'd like... _____	Ich möchte gern ... *ikh moekhter gayrn ...*
I'd like a kilo of apples, please.	Ich möchte bitte ein Kilo Äpfel *ikh moekhter bitter ain kilo epfel*
Can I...? _____	Darf ich...? *darf ikh...?*
Can I take this? _____	Darf ich dies mitnehmen? *darf ikh dees mittnaymen?*
Can I smoke here? _____	Darf ich hier rauchen? *darf ikh heer rowkhen?*
Could I ask you something?	Darf ich Sie etwas fragen? *darf ikh zee etvass fragen?*

Courtesies

Yes, of course	Ja, natürlich
	yar, natuerlikh
No, I'm sorry	Nein, es tut mir leid
	Nain, ez toot meer lait
Yes, what can I do for you?	Ja, was kann ich für Sie tun?
	yar, vass kann ikh fuer zee toon?
Just a moment, please	Einen Augenblick bitte
	ainen owgen blick bitter
No, I don't have time now	Nein, ich habe jetzt keine Zeit
	nain, ikh haber yetst kainer tsait
No, that's impossible	Nein, das ist unmöglich
	nain, dass ist oonmoeglikh
I think so	Ich glaube schon
	ikh glowber shoan
I agree	Ich glaube (es) auch
	ikh glowber (ez) owkh
I hope so too	Ich hoffe (es) auch
	ikh hoffer (ez) owkh
No, not at all	Nein, überhaupt nicht
	nain, ueberhowpt nikht
No, no-one	Nein, niemand
	nain, neemant
No, nothing	Nein, nichts
	nain, nikhts
That's (not) right	Das stimmt (nicht)
	dass shtimmt (nikht)
I (don't) agree	Da stimme ich Ihnen (nicht) zu
	dar shtimmer ikh eenen (nikht) tsoo
Okay	Einverstanden
	ain-fair-shtanden
Perhaps	vielleicht
	feelaikht
I don't know	Ich weiss es nicht
	ikh vaiss es nikht

 2.4 Thank you

Thank you	Vielen Dank
	feelen dunk
You're welcome	Keine Ursache/gern geschehen
	kainer oorzakher/gayrn geshayhen
Thank you very much	Vielen herzlichen Dank
	feelen hairtslikhen dunk
Very kind of you	Sehr freundlich (von Ihnen)
	zayr froyntlikh (fon eenen)
I enjoyed it very much	Es war mir ein Vergnügen
	es var meer ain fairgnuegen
Thank you for your trouble	Ich danke Ihnen für die Mühe
	ikh dunker eenen fuer dee muer
You shouldn't have	Das wäre nicht nötig gewesen
	dass vayrer nikht noetikh gevayzen
That's all right	Ist schon in Ordnung
	ist shoan in ordnoong

2.5 Sorry

Excuse me _____	Verzeihung
	fair tsaioong
Sorry! _____	Entschuldigung
	ent shool digoong
I'm sorry, I didn't know... ___	Entschuldigung, ich wusste nicht, dass...
	ent shool digung, ikh vuster nihkt dass...
I do apologise _____	Ich bitte vielmals um Verzeihung
	ikh bitter feelmarls oom fair tsaioong
Please don't hold _____ it against me	Nehmen Sie (es) mir bitte nicht übel
	naymen zee (es) meer bitter nikht uebel
I'm sorry _____	Es tut mir leid
	ez toot meer lait
I didn't do it on purpose, ___ it was an accident	Ich habe es nicht mit Absicht getan, es war ein Versehen
	ikh harber ez nikht mit apsikht getarn, ez var ain fairzayhen
That's all right _____	Das macht nichts
	dass makht nikhts
Never mind _____	Lassen Sie nur
	lassen zee noor
It could've happened to ___ anyone	Das kann jedem mal passieren
	dass kann yaydem marl passeeren

2.6 What do you think?

Which do you prefer? _____	Was ist Ihnen lieber?
	vass ist eenen leeber?
What do you think? _____	Was halten Sie davon?
	vass harlten zee dafonn?
I don't mind _____	Es ist mir egal
	ez ist meer egarl
Well done! _____	Sehr gut!
	zayr goot!
Not bad! _____	Nicht schlecht!
	nikht shlekht!
Great! _____	Ausgezeichnet!
	ows ge tsaykh net!
It's really nice here! _____	Hier ist es aber gemütlich!
	heer ist ez arber gemuetlikh!
How nice for you! _____	Wie hübsch/schön (für Sie/dich)!
	vee huepsh/shoen (fuer zee/dikh)!
I'm (not) very happy _____ with...	Ich bin (nicht) sehr zufrieden über...
	ikh bin (nikht) zayr tsoofreeden ueber...
I'm glad... _____	Ich bin froh, dass...
	ikh bin froa, dass...
I'm having a great time ___	Ich amüsiere mich sehr gut
	ikh amuezeerer mikh zayr goot
I'm looking forward to it ___	Ich freue mich drauf
	ikh froyer mikh drowf
Impossible _____	Unmöglich!
	oonmoeglikh!
That's terrible! _____	Wie scheußlich!
	vee shoysslikh!

What a pity! _____	Wie schade!
	vee sharder!
That's filthy! _____	Wie schmutzig/dreckig!
	vee shmootsikh/drekkikh!
What a load of rubbish! ___	(So'n) Quatsch!
	(zoan) kvatsh!
I don't like..._____	Ich mag kein/keine(n) (+ noun)/Ich (+ verb) nicht gern
	ikh mark kain/kainer(n)/ikh...nikht gayrn
I'm bored to death _____	Ich langweile mich furchtbar
	ikh langvailer mikh foorkhtbar
I've had enough_____	Mir reicht's
	meer raikhts
I was expecting _____ something completely different	Ich hatte etwas ganz anderes erwartet
	ikh hatter etvass gants andererz airvartet

Conversation

Conversation

3.1 **I** beg your pardon?

I don't speak any/ _____ I speak a little...	Ich spreche kein/ein bisschen... *ikh shprekher kain/ain bisskhen...*
I'm English _____	Ich bin Engländer/in *ikh bin englender (male)/englenderin (female)*
I'm Scottish_____	Ich bin Schotte/Schottin *ikh bin shotter/shottin*
I'm Irish _____	Ich bin Irländer/Irländerin *ikh bin earlender/earlenderin*
I'm Welsh_____	Ich bin Waliser/Waliserin *ikh bin valeezer/valeezerin*
Do you speak _____ English/French/German?	Sprechen Sie Englisch/Französisch/Deutsch? *shprekhen zee english/frantsoezish/doytsh?*
Is there anyone who_____ speaks...?	Ist hier jemand, der ... spricht? *ist heer yaymant, dayr ... shprikht?*
I beg your pardon? _____	Wie bitte? *vee bitter?*
I (don't) understand _____	Ich verstehe (es) (nicht) *ikh fair shtayher (es) (nikht)*
Do you understand me? ___	Verstehen Sie mich? *fair shtayhen zee mikh?*
Could you repeat that, ____ please?	Würden Sie das bitte wiederholen? *vuerden zee dass bitter vee-der-hoalen?*
Could you speak more_____ slowly, please?	Könnten Sie etwas langsamer sprechen? *koennten zee etvass langzarmer shprekhen?*
What does that (word) ____ mean?	Was bedeutet das/dieses Wort? *vass bedoytet dass/deezez vort?*
Is that similar to/the _____ same as...?	Ist das (ungefähr) dasselbe wie..? *ist dass (oongefair) dass zelber vee..?*
Could you write that_____ down for me, please?	Könnten Sie mir das bitte aufschreiben? *koennten zee meer dass bitter owfshraiben?*
Could you spell that _____ for me, please?	Könnten Sie mir das bitte buchstabieren? *koennten zee meer dass bitter bookhshtabeeren?*

(See 1.8 Telephone alphabet)

Could you point that_____ out in this phrase book, please?	Könnten Sie mir das in diesem Sprachführer zeigen? *koennten zee meer dass in deezem shprakhfuerer tsaigen?*
One moment, please, _____ I have to look it up	Augenblick bitte, ich muß es erst suchen *owgenblick bitte, ikh mooss ez erst zookhen*
I can't find the word/the ___ sentence	Ich kann das Wort/den Satz nicht finden *ikh kann dass vort/dayn zats nikht finden*
How do you say_____ that in...?	Wie sagt man das auf... *vee zarkt mann dass owf...*
How do you pronounce____ that?	Wie spricht man das aus? *vee shprikht mann dass ows?*

3.2 Introductions

English	German
May I introduce myself? ___	Darf ich mich Ihnen vorstellen? *darf ikh mikh eenen forshtellen?*
My name's... _____	Ich heisse... *ikh haisser...*
I'm... _____	Ich bin... *ikh bin...*
What's your name? _____	Wie heissen Sie? *vee haissen zee?*
May I introduce...? _____	Darf ich Ihnen vorstellen...? *darf ikh eenen forshtellen...?*
This is my wife/ _____ daughter/mother/ girlfriend	Dies ist meine Frau/Tochter/Mutter/Freundin *deez ist mainer frow/tokhter/mootter/froyndin*
- my husband/son/ _____ father/boyfriend	Dies ist mein Mann/Sohn/Vater/Freund. *dees ist main mann/zoan/farter/froynt.*
How do you do _____	Guten Tag/Abend, nett Sie kennenzulernen *gooten tark/arbent, nett zee kennen tsoo layrnen*
Pleased to meet you _____	Angenehm *angenaym*
Where are you from? _____	Woher kommen Sie? *voahair kommen zee?*
I'm from _____ England/Scotland/ Ireland/Wales	Ich komme aus England/Schottland/Irland/Wales *ikh kommer ows englant/shottlant/earlant/vaylz*
What city do you live in?___	In welcher Stadt wohnen Sie? *in velkher shtatt voanen zee?*
In..., It is near..._____	In.... Das ist in der Nähe von... *in.... dass ist in dayr nayher fon...*
Have you been here _____ long?	Sind Sie schon lange hier? *zint zee shoan langer heer?*
A few days _____	Ein paar Tage *ain pahr targer*
How long are you _____ staying here?	Wie lange bleiben Sie hier? *vee langer blaiben zee heer?*
We're (probably) _____ leaving tomorrow/ in two weeks	Wir reisen (wahrscheinlich) morgen/in zwei Wochen ab *veer raizen (varshainlikh) morgun/in tsvai vokhen ap*
Where are you staying?___	Wo wohnen Sie? *vo voanen zee?*
In a hotel/an apartment ___	In einem Hotel/Appartement *in ainem hotel/apartament*
On a camp site_____	Auf einem Campingplatz *owf ainem camping plats*
With friends/relatives _____	Bei Freunden/Verwandten *bai froynden/fairvanten*
Are you here on your_____ own/with your family?	Sind Sie hier allein/mit Ihrer Familie? *zint zee heer allain/mit eerer fameelyeh?*
I'm on my own_____	Ich bin allein *ikh bin allain*

Conversation

I'm with my _____ partner/wife/husband	Ich bin hier mit meinem Partner/meiner Partnerin/meiner Frau/meinem Mann
	ikh bin heer mit mainem partner/mainer partnerin/mainer frow/mainem man
– with my family _____	Ich bin hier mit mainer Familie
	ikh bin hier mit mainer fameelyeh
– with relatives _____	Ich bin hier mit Verwandten
	ikh bin hier mit fairvanten
– with a friend/friends _____	Ich bin hier mit einem Freund/einer Freundin/Freunden
	ikh bin hier mit ainem froynt/ainer froyndin/froynden
Are you married? _____	Sind Sie verheiratet?
	zint zee fairhairatet?
Do you have a steady _____ boyfriend/girlfriend?	Hast du eine feste Freundin/einen festen Freund?
	hast doo ainer fester froyndin/aynen festen froynt?
That's none of your _____ business	Das geht Sie nichts an
	dass gayt zee nikhts an
I'm married _____	Ich bin verheiratet
	ikh bin fairhai ratet
– single _____	Ich bin Junggeselle/Junggesellin
	ikh bin yoong ge zeller/yoong ge zellin
– separated _____	Ich lebe getrennt
	ikh layber getrennt
– divorced _____	Ich bin geschieden
	ikh bin gesheeden
– a widow/widower _____	Ich bin Witwe/Witwer
	ikh bin vitveh/vitver
I live alone/with _____ someone	Ich lebe allein/mit jemandem zusammen
	ikh layber allain/mit yaymandem tsoozammen
Do you have any _____ children/grandchildren?	Haben Sie Kinder/Enkel?
	harben zee kinder/enkell?
How old are you? _____	Wie alt sind Sie?
	vee alt zint zee?
How old is he/she? _____	Wie alt ist er/sie?
	vee alt ist ayr/zee?
I'm... _____	Ich bin ... Jahre alt
	ikh bin ... yahrer alt
She's/he's... _____	Sie/er ist ... Jahre alt
	zee/ayr ist ... yahrer alt
What do you do for a_____ living?	Was für eine Arbeit machen Sie?
	vass fuer ainer arbait makhen zee?
I work in an office _____	Ich arbeite in einem Büro
	ikh arbaiter in ainem buero
I'm a student/_____ I'm at school	Ich studiere/gehe zur Schule
	ikh shtoodearer/gayher tsoor shooler
I'm unemployed _____	Ich bin arbeitslos
	ikh bin arbaitsloaz
I'm retired _____	Ich bin pensioniert/Rentner/Rentnerin
	ikh bin pen zeeoa neert/rentner/rentnerin
I have taken early _____ retirement	Ich bin im Vorruhestand
	ikh bin im for-rooher-shtant
I'm on a disability _____ pension	Ich habe eine Erwerbsunfähigkeitsrente
	ikh harber ainer erverps oon fayikh kaits renter

I'm a housewife _____	Ich bin Hausfrau
	ikh bin howzfrow
Do you like your job? _____	Macht Ihnen die Arbeit Spass?
	makht eenen dee arbait shpass?
Most of the time _____	Mal ja, mal nein
	marl yar, marl nain
I usually do, but I prefer ___ holidays	Meistens schon, aber Urlaub ist schöner
	maistens shoan, arber oorlowp ist shoener

3.3 Starting/ending a conversation

Could I ask you _____ something?	Dürfte ich Sie etwas fragen?
	duerfter ikh zee etvass frargen?
Excuse me _____	Entschuldigen Sie bitte
	ent shool digen zee bitter
Excuse me, could you ____ help me?	Entschuldigung, könnten Sie mir helfen?
	ent shool digoong, koennten zee meer helfen?
Yes, what's the problem? __	Ja, was ist denn los?
	yar, vass ist den loas?
What can I do for you? ____	Was kann ich für Sie tun?
	vass kan ikh fuer zee toon?
Sorry, I don't have time ____ now	Bedaure, ich habe jetzt keine Zeit
	bedowrer, ikh harber yetst kainer tsayt
Do you have a light? _____	Haben Sie Feuer?
	harben zee foyerr?
May I join you? _____	Darf ich mich zu Ihnen setzen?
	darf ikh mikh tsoo eenen zetsen?
Could you take a _____ picture of me/us?	Würden Sie ein Foto von mir/uns machen?
	vuerden zee ain foto fon meer/oons makhen?
Leave me alone _____	Lassen Sie mich in Ruhe
	lassen zee mikh in rooher
Get lost _____	Machen Sie, daß Sie wegkommen
	makhen zee dass zee vek kommen
Go away or I'll scream ____	Wenn Sie nicht weggehen, schrei' ich
	ven zee nikht vek gayhen, shrai ikh

3.4 Congratulations and condolences

Happy birthday/many _____ happy returns	Meinen Glückwunsch zum Geburtstag
	mainen glueckvoonsh tsoom geboortstark
Please accept my _____ condolences	Mein Beileid
	main bailait
I'm very sorry for you ____	Es tut mir ja so leid für Sie
	ez toot meer yar zo lait fuer zee

3.5 A chat about the weather

See also 1.5 The weather

It's so hot/cold today! ____	Heute ist es aber warm/kalt!
	hoyter ist ez arber varm/kalt!
Nice weather, isn't it? ____	Angenehmes Wetter, nicht?
	angenaymers vetter, nikht?
What a wind/storm! _____	So ein Wind/Sturm!
	zo ain vint/shtoorm

29

All that rain/snow! _____	Wie das regnet/schneit!
	vee dass raygnet/shnait!
All that fog! _____	Das ist vielleicht ein Nebel!
	dass ist feelaikht ain naybel!
Has the weather been _____ like this for long here?	Ist das Wetter hier schon lange so?
	ist dass vetter heer shoan langer zo?
Is it always this hot/cold _____ here?	Ist es hier immer so warm/kalt?
	ist es heer immer zo varm/kalt?
Is it always this dry/wet_____ here?	Ist es hier immer so trocken/nass?
	ist es heer immer zo trokken/nass?

 .6 Hobbies

Do you have any _____ hobbies?	Haben Sie Hobbys?
	harben zee hobbies?
I like knitting/ _____ reading/photography/ painting	Ich stricke/lese/fotografiere/zeichne gern
	ikh shtrikker/layzer/fotograffearer/tsaikhner gayrn
I like music _____	Ich liebe Musik
	ikh leeber moozeek
I like playing the _____ guitar/piano	Ich spiele gern Gitarre/Klavier
	ikh shpeeler gayrn gitarrer/klaveer
I like going to the movies _____	Ich gehe gern ins Kino
	ikh gayher gayrn ins keeno
I like travelling/_____ fishing/walking/sport	Ich reise/angle/wandre gern
	ikh raizer/angler/vanderer gayrn

 .7 Being the host(ess)

See also 4 Eating out

Can I offer you a drink? _____	Darf ich Ihnen etwas zu trinken anbieten?
	darf ikh eenen etvass tsoo trinken anbeeten?
What would you like_____ to drink?	Was möchtest du trinken?
	vass moekhtest doo trinken?
Would you like a _____ cigarette/cigar?	Möchten Sie eine Zigarette/Zigarre?
	moekhten zee ainer tsigarretter/tsigarrer?
Something non-alcoholic,_____ please	Gern etwas ohne Alkohol
	gayrn etvass oaner alkohol
I don't smoke _____	Ich rauche nicht
	ikh rowkher nikht

 .8 Invitations

Are you doing anything_____ tonight?	Hast du heute abend was vor?
	hast doo hoyter arbent vass for?
Do you have any plans _____ for today/this afternoon/tonight?	Haben Sie schon Pläne für heute/heute nachmittag/heute abend?
	harben zee shoan playner fuer hoyter/hoyter nakhmittark/hoyter arbent?
Would you like to go _____ out with me?	Haben Sie Lust, mit mir auszugehen?
	harben zee loost, mit meer ows tsoo gayhen?
Would you like to go _____ dancing with me?	Haben Sie Lust, mit mir tanzen zu gehen?
	harben zee loost, mitt meer tantsen tsoo gayhen?

Would you like to have ____ lunch/dinner with me?	Haben Sie Lust, mit mir zu essen?
	harben zee loost, mit meer tsoo essen?
Would you like to come____ to the beach with me?	Haben Sie Lust, an den Strand zu gehen?
	harben zee loost, an den shtrant tsoo gayhen?
Would you like to come____ into town with us?	Haben Sie Lust, mit uns in die Stadt zu gehen/fahren?
	harben zee loost, mit oons in dee shtatt tsoo gayhen/fahren?
Would you like to come____ and see some friends with us?	Haben Sie Lust, mit uns zu Freunden zu gehen?
	harben zee loost, mit oons tsoo froynden tsoo gayhen?
Shall we dance?_____	Wollen wir tanzen?
	vollen veer tantsen?
– sit at the bar? _____	Kommst du mit an die Bar?
	kommst doo mit an dee bar?
– get something to drink? __	Wollen wir etwas trinken?
	vollen veer etvass trinken?
– go for a walk/drive?_____	Wollen wir ein bisschen spazierengehen/Auto fahren?
	vollen veer ain bisskhen shpatseeren gayhen/owto fahren?
Yes, all right _____	Ja, gut
	yar, goot
Good idea _____	Gute Idee
	gooter eeday
No (thank you) _____	Nein (danke)
	nain (dunker)
Maybe later_____	Vielleicht später
	feelaikht shpayter
I don't feel like it _____	Dazu habe ich keine Lust
	datsoo harber ikh kainer loost
I don't have time _____	Ich habe keine Zeit
	ikh harber kainer tsait
I already have a date _____	Ich habe schon eine Verabredung
	ikh harber shoan ainer fair ap ray doong
I'm not very good at_____ dancing/volleyball/ swimming	Ich kann nicht tanzen/Volleyball spielen/schwimmen
	ikh kann nikht tantsen/volleyball shpeelen/shvimmen

3 .9 Paying a compliment

You look wonderful! _____	Sie sehen (ja) fabelhaft aus!
	zee zayhen (yar) farbelhaft ows!
I like your car! _____	Schönes/tolles Auto!
	shoenez/tollez owto!
I like your ski outfit! _____	Hübscher Skianzug!
	huepsher shee antsook!
You're a nice boy/girl _____	Du bist lieb
	doo bist leep
What a sweet child! _____	Was für ein liebes Kind!
	vass fuer ain leebes kint!
You're a wonderful _____ dancer!	Sie tanzen sehr gut!
	zee tantsen zayr goot!

You're a wonderful cook!	Sie kochen sehr gut!
	zee kokhen zayr goot!
You're a terrific soccer player!	Sie spielen sehr gut Fussball!
	zee shpeelen zayr goot foossball!

⒊.10 Chatting someone up

I like being with you	Ich bin gern mit dir zusammen
	ikh bin gayrn mit deer tsoozammen
I've missed you so much	Ich habe dich so vermisst
	ikh haber dikh zo fairmisst
I dreamt about you	Ich habe von dir geträumt
	ikh haber fon deer getroymt
I think about you all day	Ich muss den ganzen Tag an dich denken
	ikh muss den gantsen tark an dikh denken
You have such a sweet smile	Du lächelst so süss
	doo laekhelst zo suess
You have such beautiful eyes	Du hast so schöne Augen
	doo hast zo shoener owgen
I'm in love with you	Ich habe mich in dich verliebt
	ikh haber mikh in dikh fairleept
I'm in love with you too	Ich mich auch in dich
	ikh mikh owkh in dikh
I love you	Ich liebe dich
	ikh leeber dikh
I love you too	Ich dich auch
	ikh dikh owkh
I don't feel as strongly about you	Ich empfinde nicht dasselbe für dich
	ikh empfinder nikht dass selber fuer dikh
I already have a boyfriend/girlfriend	Ich habe schon einen Freund/eine Freundin
	ikh harber shoan ainen froynt/ainer froyndin
I'm not ready for that	Ich bin noch nicht so weit
	ikh bin nokh nikht zo vait
This is going too fast for me	Es geht mir viel zu schnell
	ez gayt meer feel tsoo shnell
Take your hands off me	Rühr mich nicht an
	ruehr mikh nikht an
Okay, no problem	O.k., kein Problem
	oakay, kain problaym
Will you stay with me tonight?	Bleibst du heute nacht bei mir?
	blaipst doo hoyter nakht bai meer?
I'd like to go to bed with you	Ich möchte mit dir schlafen
	ikh moekhter mit deer shlarfen
Only if we use a condom	Nur mit Präservativ/Kondom
	noor mitt prezervatif/kondoam
We have to be careful about AIDS	Wir müssen vorsichtig sein wegen Aids
	veer muessen forsikhtikh zain vaygen aids
That's what they all say	Das sagen alle
	dass zargen aller
We shouldn't take any risks	Wir wollen lieber kein Risiko eingehen
	veer vollen leeber kain reeziko aingayhen
Do you have a condom?	Hast du ein Präservativ/Kondom?
	hast doo ain prezervatif/kondoam?
No? In that case we won't do it	Nein? Dann machen wir's nicht
	nain? dann makhen veer's nikht

.11 Arrangements

When will I see you again?	Wann sehe ich Sie/dich wieder? *vann zayher ikh zee/dikh veeder?*
Are you free over the weekend?	Haben Sie am Wochenende Zeit? *harben zee am vokhenender tsait?*
What shall we arrange?	Wie verbleiben wir? *vee fairblaiben veer?*
Where shall we meet?	Wo wollen wir uns treffen? *voa vollen veer oons treffen?*
Will you pick me/us up?	Holen Sie mich/uns ab? *hoalen zee mikh/oons ap?*
Shall I pick you up?	Soll ich Sie abholen? *zoll ikh zee apholen?*
I have to be home by...	Ich muss um...Uhr zu Hause sein *ikh muss oom...ooer tsoo howzer zain*
I don't want to see you anymore	Ich will Sie nicht mehr sehen *ikh vill zee nikht mayr zayhen*

.12 Saying goodbye

Can I take you home?	Darf ich Sie nach Hause bringen? *darf ikh zee nakh howzer bringen?*
Can I write/call you?	Darf ich Ihnen schreiben/Sie anrufen? *darf ikh eenen shraiben/zee anroofen?*
Will you write/call me?	Schreiben Sie mir/rufen Sie mich an? *shraiben zee meer/roofen zee mikh an?*
Can I have your address/phone number?	Geben Sie mir Ihre Adresse/Telefonnummer? *gayben zee meer eerer adresser/telefoan noomer?*
Thanks for everything	Vielen Dank für alles *feelen dunk fuer alless*
It was very nice	Es war sehr schön *es var zayr shoen*
Say hello to...	Grüssen Sie... *gruessen zee...*
All the best	Alles Gute *alles gooter*
Good luck	Viel Erfolg weiter *feel erfolk vaiter*
When will you be back?	Wann kommst du wieder? *vann kommst doo veeder?*
I'll be waiting for you	Ich warte auf dich *ikh varter owf dikh*
I'd like to see you again	Ich möchte dich gern wiedersehen *ikh moekhter dikh gayrn veeder zayhen*
I hope we meet again soon	Ich hoffe, wir sehen uns wieder *ikh hoffer, veer zayhen oons veeder*
This is our address. If you're ever in the UK...	Dies ist unsere Adresse. Wenn Sie je in Grossbritannien sind... *deez ist oonzerer adresser. venn zee yay in englant zint...*
You'd be more than welcome	Sie sind uns herzlich willkommen *zee zint oons hertslikh villkommen*

Conversation

Eating out

4 Eating out

● **In Germany** people usually have three main meals:
1 *Frühstück* (breakfast) between approx. 6.30 and 10 am. Breakfast is varied and can consist of coffee or herbal infusions, cereal (particularly muesli), bread rolls or slices of *Vollkornbrot* (whole-wheat bread) with a choice of butter, jam, ham or cheese. On Sundays this array is often complemented by boiled eggs.
2 *Mittagessen* (lunch) approx. between midday and 2 pm. Traditionally lunch consists of a hot dish and is the most important meal of the day. Offices and shops often close while lunch is taken at home, in a restaurant or canteen. It usually consists of two or three courses:
– starter
– main course
– dessert
3 *Abendessen* (dinner)/*Vesper* (cold evening meal in southern Germany) between 6 and 9.30 pm. This either consists of a light hot meal or a cold meal such as slices of bread with cold meat, cheese and salad.

4.1 On arrival

I'd like to book a table for seven o'clock, please	Kann ich einen Tisch für sieben Uhr reservieren lassen? *kann ikh ainen tish fuer zeeben ooer rezerveeren lassen?*
I'd like a table for two, please	Bitte einen Tisch für zwei Personen *bitter ainen tish fuer tsvai perzoanen*
We've/we haven't booked	Wir haben (nicht) reserviert *veer harben (nikht) rezerveert*
Is the restaurant open yet?	Hat die Küche schon geöffnet? *hat dee kuekher shoan geoeffnet?*
What time does the restaurant open/close?	Wann öffnet/schliesst die Küche? *vann oeffnet/shleest dee kuekher?*
Can we wait for a table?	Können wir auf einen Tisch warten? *koennen veer owf ainen tish varten?*
Do we have to wait long?	Müssen wir lange warten? *muessen veer langer varten?*

Haben Sie reserviert?	Do you have a reservation?
Unter welchem Namen?	What name, please?
Hierher bitte	This way, please
Dieser Tisch ist reserviert	This table is reserved
In einer Viertelstunde wird ein Tisch frei	We'll have a table free in fifteen minutes
Möchten Sie solange (an der Bar) warten?	Would you like to wait (at the bar)?

Is this seat taken?	Ist dieser Platz frei? *ist deezer plats frai?*
Could we sit here/there?	Können wir uns hierher/dahin setzen? *koennen veer oons heerhair/darhin zetzen?*
Can we sit by the window?	Können wir uns ans Fenster setzen? *koennen veer oons ans fenster zetzen?*

Eating out

Can we eat outside? _____	Können wir auch draussen essen?
	koennen veer owkh drowsen essen?
Do you have another _____ chair for us?	Könnten Sie uns noch einen Stuhl bringen?
	koennten zee oons nokh ainen shtool bringen?
Do you have a highchair? __	Könnten Sie uns einen Kinderstuhl bringen?
	koennten zee oons ainen kindershtool bringen?
Is there a socket for _____ this bottle-warmer?	Gibt es für diesen Flaschenwärmer eine Steckdose?
	gipt es fuer deezen flashen vayrmerr ainer shtekdozer?
Could you warm up _____ this bottle/jar for me?	Könnten Sie mir dieses Fläschchen/Gläschen aufwärmen?
	koennten zee meer deezez fleshkhen/glayzkhen owfvermen?
Not too hot, please _____	Nicht zu heiss bitte
	nikht tsoo haiss bitter
Is there somewhere I _____ can change the baby's nappy?	Gibt es hier einen Raum, wo ich das Baby wickeln kann?
	gipt ez heer ainen rowm vo ikh dass bayby vikkeln kann?
Where are the toilets? _____	Wo ist die Toilette?
	vo ist dee twaletter?

4.2 Ordering

Waiter! _____	Herr Ober!
	herr oaber!
Madam! _____	Bedienung!
	bedeenoong!
Sir! _____	Bitte!
	bitter!
We'd like something to ___ eat/a drink	Wir möchten gern etwas essen/trinken
	veer moekhten gayrn etvass essen/trinken
Could I have a quick _____ meal?	Könnte ich schnell etwas essen?
	koennter ikh shnell etvass essen?
We don't have much time__	Wir haben wenig Zeit
	veer harben vaynikh tsait
We'd like to have a _____ drink first	Wir möchten erst noch etwas trinken
	veer moekhten ayrst nokh etvass trinken
Could we see the _____ menu/wine list, please?	Wir hätten gern die Speisekarte/Weinkarte/(Getränkekarte)
	veer hetten gayrn dee spaizer karter/vain karter(gertrenker karte)
Do you have a menu _____ in English?	Haben Sie eine Speisekarte in Englisch?
	harben zee ainer shpayzer karter in english?
Do you have a dish _____ of the day?	Haben Sie ein Tagesmenü/Touristenmenü?
	harben zee ain targes menyoo/toorissten menyoo?
We haven't made a _____ choice yet	Wir haben noch nicht gewählt
	veer harben nokh nikht gevaylt
What do you _____ recommend?	Was können Sie uns empfehlen?
	vass koennen zee oons empfaylen?

What are the specialities of the region/the house?	Welches sind die Spezialitäten dieser Gegend/des Hauses?
	velkhes zint dee shpetseeali tayten deezer gegent/dez howzez?
I like strawberries/olives	Ich liebe Erdbeeren/Oliven
	ikh leeber ertbeeren/olleeven
I don't like meat/fish/...	Ich mag kein Fleisch/keinen Fisch
	ikh mark kain flaish/kainen fish
What's this?	Was ist das?
	vass ist dass?
Does it have...in it?	Ist das mit...?
	ist dass mit...?
What does it taste like?	Womit kann man das vergleichen?
	vo-mitt kann mann dass fairglaikhen?
Is this a hot or a cold dish?	Ist dieses Gericht warm oder kalt?
	ist deezes gerikht varm oader kalt?
Is this sweet?	Ist es eine Süßspeise?
	ist ez ainer suess shpaizer?
Is this spicy?	Ist es pikant/scharf?
	ist es peekant/sharf?
Do you have anything else, please?	Haben Sie vielleicht etwas anderes?
	harben zee feelaihkt etvass anderez?
I'm on a salt-free diet	Ich darf kein Salz essen
	ikh darf kain zalts essen
I can't eat pork	Ich darf kein Schweinefleisch essen
	ikh darf kain shvainer flaish essen
– sugar	Ich darf keinen Zucker essen
	ikh darf kainen tsooker essen
– fatty foods	Ich darf kein Fett essen
	ikh darf kain fet essen
– (hot) spices	Ich darf keine scharfen Gewürze essen
	ikh darf kainer sharfen gewuertser essen
I'll/we'll have what those people are having	Ich möchte/wir möchten gern dasselbe wie die Leute da
	ikh moekhter/veer moekhten gayrn dass selber vee dee loyter dar
I'd like...	Ich möchte...
	ikh moekhter...
We're not having a starter	Wir nehmen keine Vorspeise
	veer naymen kainer for shpaizer

Eating out

Möchten Sie essen/speisen?	Would you like to eat?
Haben Sie schon gewählt?	Have you decided?
Möchten Sie eine Nachspeise?	Would you like a dessert?
Was darf es sein?	What would you like?
Guten Appetit!	Enjoy your meal
Darf/Dürfte ich jetzt abrechnen?	May I ask you to settle the bill, please?

The child will share_____ what we're having	Das Kind isst etwas von unserem Menü mit *dass kint ist etvass fon oonzerem menyoo mit*
Could I have some _____ more bread, please?	Noch etwas Brot bitte *nokh etvass broat bitter*
– a bottle of water/wine ___	Noch eine Flasche (Mineral)wasser/Wein bitte *nokh ainer flasher (minerarl)vasser/vain bitter*
– another helping of... _____	Noch eine Portion....bitte *nokh ainer portseeoan...bitter*
– some salt and pepper ___	Würden Sie bitte Salz und Pfeffer bringen? *vuerden zee bitter zalts unt pfeffer bringen?*
– a napkin _____	Würden Sie bitte eine Serviette bringen? *vuerden zee bitter ainer zerviyetter bringen?*
– a spoon_____	Würden Sie bitte einen Löffel bringen? *vuerden zee bitter ainen loeffel bringen?*
– an ashtray _____	Würden Sie bitte einen Aschenbecher bringen? *vuerden zee bitter ainen ashen bekher bringen?*
– some matches_____	Würden Sie bitte Streichhölzer bringen? *vuerden zee bitter shtraikh hoeltser bringen?*
– a glass of water _____	Würden Sie bitte ein Glas Wasser bringen? *vuerden zee bitter ain glars vasser bringen?*
– a straw (for the child) ___	Würden Sie bitte (für das Kind) einen Trinkhalm bringen? *vuerden zee bitter (fuer dass kint) ainen trinkhalm bringen?*
Enjoy your meal!_____	Guten Appetit! *gooten appeteet!*
You too! _____	Danke, gleichfalls *dunker, glaikhfals*
Cheers!_____	Prost/zum Wohl! *prrosst/tsoom voal!*
The next round's on me ___	Die nächste Runde gebe ich (aus) *dee nexter roonder gayber ikh (ows)*
Could we have a doggy____ bag, please?	Dürfen wir die Reste mitnehmen? *duerfen veer dee rester mitnaymen?*

4 .3 The bill

See also 8.2 Settling the bill

How much is this dish? ____	Wieviel kostet dieses Gericht? *veefeel kostet deezes gerikht?*
Could I have the bill, _____ please?	Die Rechnung bitte *dee rekhnoong bitter*
All together _____	Alles zusammen *alles tsoozammen*
Everyone pays separately __	Getrennt zahlen *getrennt tsarlen*

Could we have the menu __ again, please?	Dürften wir die Karte noch mal sehen? *duerften veer dee karter nokh marl zayhen?*
The...is not on the bill ____	Der/die/das...steht nicht auf der Rechnung *der/dee/dass...shtayt nihkt owf dayr rekhnoong*

4 .4 Complaints

It's taking a very_____ long time	Das dauert aber lange *dass dowert arber langer*
We've been here an _____ hour already	Wir sitzen hier schon seit einer Stunde *veer zitsen heer shoan zait ainer shtoonder*
This must be a mistake ___	Das muss ein Irrtoom sein *dass muss ain eartoom zain*
This is not what I_____ ordered	Das habe ich nicht bestellt *dass harber ikh nikht beshtellt*
I ordered..._____	Ich habe um...gebeten *ikh harber oom...gebayten*
There's a dish missing_____	Es fehlt ein Gericht *ez faylt ain gerikht*
This is broken/not clean ___	Das ist kaputt/nicht sauber *dass ist kapoott/nikht zowber*
The food's cold _____	Das Essen ist kalt *dass essen ist kalt*
– not fresh _____	Das Essen ist nicht frisch *dass essen ist nikht frish*
– too salty/sweet/spicy_____	Das Essen ist versalzen/zu süss/scharf *dass essen ist fairzaltsen/tsoo zuess/sharf*
The meat's not done_____	Das Fleisch ist nicht gar *dass flaish ist nikht garr*
– overdone _____	Das Fleisch ist zu sehr durchgebraten *dass flaish ist tsoo zayr doorkh gebrarten*
– tough _____	Das Fleisch ist zäh *dass flaish ist tsay*
– off _____	Das Fleisch ist verdorben *dass flaish ist fairdorben*
Could I have something ___ else instead of this?	Können Sie mir hierfür etwas anderes bringen? *koennen zee meer heerfuerr etvass anderez bringen?*
The bill/this amount is_____ not right	Die Rechnung/dieser Betrag stimmt nicht *dee rekhnoong/deezer betrark shtimmt nikht*
We didn't have this_____	Das haben wir nicht gehabt *dass harben veer nihkt gehapt*
There's no paper in the ___ toilet	Auf der Toilette ist kein Toilettenpapier *owf der twaletter ist kain twaletten papeer*
Do you have a _____ complaints book?	haben Sie ein Beschwerdebuch *harben zee ain beshverder bookh?*
Will you call the_____ manager, please?	Würden Sie bitte den Chef rufen? *vuerden zee bitter den shef roofen?*

.5 Paying a compliment

That was a wonderful _____ Wir haben herrlich gegessen
  meal   *veer harben hairlikh gegessen*
The food was excellent _____ Es hat uns ausgezeichnet geschmeckt
    ez hat oons owsge tsaikhnet geshmekt
The...in particular was _____ Vor allem der/die/das...war hervorragend
  delicious   *for allem dayr/dee/dass...var hair for rargent*

.6 The menu

Bedienung einschliesslich
service included
Beilagen
side-dishes
Erfrischungsgetränke
refreshment drinks
Fisch
fish
Frühstück
breakfast
Gebäck
biscuits, pastries, buns, tarts, tartlets
Gedeck
set meal/place
Gerichte
dishes

Getränke (karte)
beverages/list of beverages (café) or wine list (restaurant)
Happen
snack
Hauptgerichte
main courses
Köstlichkeiten
delicacies
Kuchen
cake(s)
Meeresfrüchte
seafood
Nachspeisen
desserts
Spezialitäten
specialities

Suppen
soups
Tagesmenü
menu of the day
Tagesteller
dish of the day
Torten
gateau/flan (with fruit)
Vorspeisen
starters
Weine
wines
Weinkarte
wine list
Zwischengerichte
entrée/snack

.7 Alphabetical list of drinks and dishes

Aal
eel
Apfel
apple
Äpfel im Schlafrock
baked apples in puff pastry
Apfelsine
orange
Aspik
aspic
Aufschnitt
sliced cold meat or (rarer) cheese
Austern
oysters
Bauern-
farmer's/rustic
-brot
coarse rye bread

-frühstück
bacon and potato omelette
Beeren
berries
Birne
pears
Bismarckhering
Bismarck herring (filleted pickled herring)
Blaubeere
blueberry
Blaukraut
red cabbage
Bohnen (grüne, grosse)
green beans
Braten
roast

Bratkartoffeln
fried potatoes
Brause
pop/lemonade
Bries(chen), Briesel
dish containing sweetbreads of animals (mostly calves)
Brombeere
blackberry
Brot
bread
Brötchen
bread rolls
Brühe
clear soup/stock
Brust
breast

Bündner Fleisch
smoked ham from the region of Graubünden in Switzerland
Butt
flounder/butt
Butter
butter
Chicoree
chicory
Curry
curry
Dampfnudeln
sweet yeast dumpling cooked in milk and sugar
Dattel
date
Dörr-
dried
Dorsch
cod
Eierkuchen (dünn)
(thin) pancakes
Eierstich
egg based ingredient of some soups
Eintopf
stew
Eisbecher
sundae(s)
Eisbombe
ice cream cake
Endivie
endive
Ente
duck
Erbsen
peas
Erdbeere
strawberry
Essig
vinegar
Fadennudeln
vermicelli
Feige
fig
Filetsteak
fillet steak
Fisch
fish
Fisolen
green beans
Fleisch
meat

Flusskrebs
crayfish
Frikassee (Hühner-)
(chicken) fricassee
Frittatensuppe
soup containing strips of pancake
Frühlingsrolle
spring rolls
Gänseleber
goose liver
Garnele
shrimp
gebraten
fried
gedünstet
braised
Geflügel
poultry
gefüllt
filled/stuffed
gekocht
boiled
Gelee
jelly
Gemüse
vegetables
geräuchert
smoked
Geschnetzeltes
meat cut into strips stewed to produce a thick sauce
Geselchtes
salted and smoked meat
gespickt
larded/fried meat with strips of bacon
getrocknet
dried
gewürzt
seasoned
Glühwein
mulled wine
Grog
grog
Gulasch
goulash
Gurke (saure-)
(pickled) gherkins
Hähnchen/Hühnchen
chicken
Hase
hare

Haselnuss
hazelnut
Hasenpfeffer
jugged hare
Hering
herring
Heurige(r)
new wine
Himbeere
raspberry
Hirn
brains
Hirsch
venison
Hummer
lobster
Ingwer
ginger
Jause
snack
Johannisbeere
blackcurrant/redcurrant
Kalb
calf
Kaldaunen/Kutteln
tripe
Kaltschale
cold sweet soup
Kaninchen
rabbit
Karfiol
cauliflower
Karotten
carrots
Karpfen
carp
Kartoffel
potato
Kartoffelpuffer
potato fritter
Käse
cheese
Kekse
biscuits
Keule
leg
Kirsche
cherry
Klösse (Kartoffel-, Semmel-)
dumplings (potato, bread)
Knoblauch
garlic
Knödel
dumplings

Knusprig
crisp/crunchy
Kochschinken
boiled ham
Kompott
stewed fruit/compote
Konfitüre
jam
Korn
corn/corn schnapps
Krabbe
crab
Krapfen
doughnut
Kräuter-
herbal
Labskaus
stew made of meat,
 fish and mashed
 potato
Lachs
salmon
Languste
crayfish
Lauch
leek
Lebkuchen
gingerbread
Likör
liqueur
Mandel
almond
Marille
apricot
mariniert
marinated
Marone
chestnut
Maultaschen
filled pasta squares
Meerrettich
horseradish
Melone
melon
Mett
minced pork/beef
Milch
milk
Muscheln
mussels
Nockerl
little dumplings
Nougat
nougat

Obst (je nach
 Jahreszeit/Saison)
fruit (of the season)
Obstkuchen
fruitcake
Obstler
fruit schnapps
Ochsenschwanz
oxtail
Öl
oil
Orange
orange
Palatschinken
stuffed pancake
Pampelmuse
grapefruit
Pastete
paté
Petersilie
parsley
Pfannkuchen
pancake
Pfeffer
pepper
Pfifferling
chanterelle
Pfirsich
peach
Pflaume
plum
Pilze
mushrooms
Platte
plate
Plätzchen
biscuit/cookie
Pommes frites
French fries
Porree
leek
Preßsack
a type of cold meat
Pute
turkey
Quark
(soft) curd cheese
Radieschen
radish
Rahm
cream
Räucherschinken
smoked ham
Rebhuhn
partridge

Reh
deer
Reibekuchen
potato waffle
Reis
rice
Remoulade
remoulade
resch (rösch)
crisp/crusty
Rinder-
beef
Rinderfilet
beef fillet
Rindfleisch
beef
Rippe
rib
roh
raw
Rosenkohl
Brussels sprouts
Rosine
raisin
Rostbraten
roast
Röstkartoffeln
fried potatoes
rote Beete
beetroot
Rührei
scrambled eggs
Rumpsteak
rump steak
Sachertorte
a rich chocolate cake
Saft
juice
Sahne
cream
Salat (gemischt)
salad (mixed)
Salzkartoffeln
boiled potatoes
Sauerkraut
sauerkraut/pickled
 cabbage
Schaum-
frothy
Schildkrötensuppe
turtle soup
Schinken
ham
Schlagobers
whipped cream

Schmalz
lard
Schmarren
pancake cut up into
  small pieces
Schnecken
escargots
Schnittchen (Appe-
tit)
canapé
Schnittlauch
chives
Schorle
wine and soda water
  mix
Schweinefleisch
pork
Schweinelendchen
small pieces of pork
loin
Sekt
sparkling wine
Sellerie
celery
Semmel
bread roll
Senf
mustard
Sosse
gravy/sauce
Spanferkel
whole pig roasted
  over an open fire
Spargel
asparagus
Spätzle
spaetzle (type of
  pasta)

Speiseeis
ice-cream
Spinat
spinach
Steinpilz
type of mushroom
  (*Boletus edulis*)
Strammer Max
open sandwich of
  boiled ham and
  fried egg
Strudel
strudel
Süßspeise
sweet dish
Teig (in Öl gebacken)
pastry, batter (baked
  in oil)
Thunfisch
tuna
Tintenfisch
cuttlefish/squid
Topfen
soft curd cheese
Traube
grape
Truthahn
turkey
Tunke
sauce/gravy
Vesper
a break for
  eating/cold evening
  meal
Wachtel
quail
Wald-
forest

Walnuss
walnut
Wein (trocken/mild)
wine (dry/mild)
Wein (süss/
Spätlese/Eiswein)
wine (sweet/late
  vintage/sweet wine
  made from grapes
  which have been
  exposed to frost)
Wein (Süsswein/
  Südwein)
wine (dessert
  wine/
  Mediterranean wine)
Weinbrand
brandy
Weisswurst
veal sausage
Wels
catfish
Würstchen
sausage
Zitrone
lemon
Zunge
tongue
Zwiebel
onion

On the road

5 On the road

5.1 Asking for directions

Excuse me, could I ask you something?	Verzeihung, dürfte ich Sie etwas fragen? *fair tsaioong, duerfter ikh zee etvass frargen?*
I've lost my way	Ich habe mich verlaufen/(with car)mich verfahren *ikh harber mikh fairlowfen/mikh fairfahren*
Is there a(n)... around here?	Wissen Sie, wo hier in der Nähe ein(e)... ist? *vissen zee, vo heer in dayr nayher ain(er)... ist?*
Is this the way to...?	Ist dies die Strasse nach...? *ist dees dee shtrasser nakh...?*
Could you tell me how to get to the... (name of place) by car/on foot?	Können Sie mir sagen, wie ich nach... (name of the place) fahren/gehen muss? *koenen zee meer zargen, vee ikh nakh ... fahren/gayhen muss?*
What's the quickest way to...?	Wie komme ich am schnellsten nach...? *vee kommer ikh am shnellsten nakh...?*
How many kilometres is it to...?	Wieviel Kilometer sind es noch bis...? *veefeel kilomayter zint ez nokh biss...?*
Could you point it out on the map?	Können Sie es mir auf der Karte zeigen? *koennen zee ez meer owf dayr karter tsaigen?*

Ich weiss nicht, ich kenne mich hier nicht aus	I don't know, I don't know my way around here
Da sind Sie hier nicht richtig	You're going the wrong way
Sie müssen zurück nach...	You have to go back to...
Sie fahren über die...Strasse	You take...Street
Sie fahren über die...Strasse drüber	You cross over...Street
Da sehen Sie schon die Schilder	From there on you will see the signs
Da müssen Sie noch mal fragen	When you get there, you will have to ask again

geradeaus **straight**	überqueren **cross**	der Fluss **the river**
nach links/links abbiegen **left/turn left**	die Kreuzung **the intersection**	die Brücke **the bridge**
nach rechts/rechts abbiegen **right/turn right**	die Strasse **the street**	die (Bahn)schranken **the level crossing/ the boomgates**
abbiegen **turn**	die (Verkehrs)ampel **the traffic light**	das Schild Richtung ... **the sign pointing to ...**
folgen **follow**	das Gebäude **the building**	der Pfeil **the arrow**
	an der Ecke **at the corner**	

5.2 Customs

● **Border documents** Germany: valid passport. For car and motorbike: valid UK driving licence and registration document, insurance document, green card, UK registration plate, country identification sticker on the back of the car, First Aid kit containing sterile gloves. Caravan: must be entered on the green card, country identification sticker must be visible. A warning triangle, headlight convertors and extra headlamp bulbs must be carried.
Import and export specifications:
Foreign currency: no restrictions
With the single European Market, travellers are only subject to selective spot checks. There is no restriction, either by quantity or value, on goods purchased by travellers in another EC country provided they are for their own personal use. However, guidelines have been published. As these are subject to change you are advised to contact your travel agent, customs or the Embassy for further details before travelling.

Ihren Pass bitte _____	Your passport, please
Die grüne Karte bitte _____	Your green card, please
Ihre Fahrzeugpapiere bitte _____	Your vehicle documents, please
Ihr Visum bitte_____	Your visa, please
Wohin fahren Sie? _____	Where are you heading?
Wie lange bleiben Sie/halten Sie _____ sich dort auf?	How long are you planning to stay?
Haben Sie etwas zu verzollen? _____	Do you have anything to declare?
Würden Sie dies bitte öffnen? _____	Open this, please

My children are entered ___ on this passport	Meine Kinder sind in diesem Pass eingetragen
	mainer kinder zint in deezem parss ain getrargen
I'm travelling through _____	Ich bin auf der Durchreise
	ikh bin owf dayr doorkh raizer
I'm going on holiday to... __	*Ich fahre in den Urlaub nach...*
	ikh fahrer in den oorlowp nakh...
I'm on a business trip _____	Ich bin auf Geschäftsreise
	ikh bin owf geshefts raizer
I don't know how long_____ I'll be staying yet	Ich weiss noch nicht, wie lange ich bleibe
	ikh vaiss nokh nikht, vee langer ikh blaiber
I'll be staying here for _____ a weekend	Ich bleibe hier übers Wochenende
	ikh blaiber heer uebers vokhen ender
– for a few days _____	Ich bleibe hier ein paar Tage
	ikh blaiber heer ain par targer
– for a week_____	Ich bleibe hier eine Woche
	ikh blaiber heer ainer vokher
– for two weeks _____	Ich bleibe hier zwei Wochen
	ikh blaiber heer tsvai vokhen
I've got nothing to_____ declare	Ich habe nichts zu verzollen
	ikh harber nikhts tsoo fairtsollen

I've got...with me _____	Ich habe ... mit
	ikh harber ... mit
– a carton of cigarettes ____	Ich habe eine Stange Zigaretten
	ikh harber ainer shtanger tseegaretten
– a bottle of... _____	Ich habe eine Flasche...
	ikh harber ainer flusher...
– some souvenirs _____	Ich habe ein paar Andenken
	ikh harber ain par andenken
These are personal _____ effects	Das sind persönliche Sachen
	dass zint perzoenlikher zakhen
These are not new _____	Diese Sachen sind nicht neu
	deezer zakhen zint nikht noy
Here's the receipt _____	Hier ist der (Kassen)zettel
	heer ist dayr (kassen)tsettel
This is for private use ____	Das ist für den eigenen Gebrauch
	dass ist fuer dayn aigenen gebrowkh
How much import duty ____ do I have to pay?	Wieviel Einfuhrzoll muss ich zahlen?
	veefeel ainfoor tsoll muss ikh tsarlen?
Can I go now? _____	Darf ich jetzt gehen?
	darf ikh yetst gayhen?
Porter! _____	Gepäckträger!
	gepeck trayger!
Could you take this _____ luggage to...?	Würden Sie dieses Gepäck zu/in... bringen?
	vuerden zee deezes gepek tsoo/in... bringen?

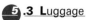 .3 Luggage

How much do I _____ owe you?	Wieviel bekommen Sie von mir?
	veefeel bekommen zee fon meer?
Where can I find a _____ luggage trolley?	Wo kann ich eine Gepäckkarre finden?
	vo kann ikh ainer gepek karrer finden?
Could you store this _____ luggage for me?	Kann ich dieses Gepäck zur Aufbewahrung abgeben?
	kann ikh deezes gepek tsoor owfbevahrung apgayben?
Where are the luggage ____ lockers?	Wo sind die Schliessfächer?
	vo zint dee shleess fekher?
I can't get the locker _____ open	Ich bekomme das Schliessfach nicht auf
	ikh bekommer dass shleessfakh nikht owf
How much is it per item ____ per day?	Wieviel kostet es je Stück pro Tag?
	veefeel kostet es yay shtuek pro tark?
This is not my bag/_____ suitcase	Das ist nicht meine Tasche/mein Koffer
	dass ist nikht mainer tasher/main koffer
There's one item/bag/ _____ suitcase missing still	Es fehlt noch ein Stück/eine Tasche/ein Koffer
	ez faylt nokh ain shtuek/ayner tasher/ain koffer
My suitcase is damaged ____	Mein Koffer ist beschädigt
	main koffer ist beshaydikt

abbiegen
turn
Anlieger frei
residents only
Auffahrt
slip road/approach
 to house
Auflieger schwenkt
 aus
trailer may swing
 out
Ausfahrt
exit
Autobahndreieck
motorway merging
 point
Baustelle
road works ahead
bei Nässe/Glätte
in wet -/icy
 conditions
Durchgangsverkehr
 (verboten)
(no) throughway
Einbahnstrasse
one way street
Einfahrt
entry/access
Ende der Autobahn
end of motorway
Frostaufbrüche
frost damage
Gefahr
danger
gefährlich
dangerous
Gegenverkehr
oncoming traffic

gesperrt (für alle
 Fahrzeuge)
closed (for all
 vehicles)
Glatteis
ice on road
Kurve(nreiche
 Strecke)
bend/dangerous
 bends
Licht einschalten/
 ausschalten
switch on lights/end
 needs for lights
LKW
heavy goods vehicle
Naturschutzgebiet
nature reserve
Nebel
beware fog
Parkscheibe
parking disk
PKW
motorcar
Radfahrer kreuzen
cyclists crossing
Rasthof-stätte
services
Rastplatz bitte
 sauberhalten
please keep picnic
 area tidy
Rollsplit
loose chippings
Schleudergefahr
danger of skidding
Seitenstreifen nicht
 befahrbar
soft verges

Seitenwind
crosswind
Spurrillen
irregular road
 surface
Standstreifen
hard shoulder
Starkes Gefälle
steep hill
Stau
traffic jam
Stauwarnanlage
hazard lights
Steinschlag
falling stones
Talbrücke
bridge over a valley
Überholverbot
no overtaking
Umleitung
diversion
Unbeschränkter
 Bahnübergang
unguarded level
 crossing/dangerous
 crossing
Verengte Fahrbahn
narrow lane
Vorfahrt beachten
give way
Vorfahrtsstrasse
major road
Wasserschutzgebiet
protected reservoir
 area
zurückschalten
to change back

.5 The car

See the diagram on page 51.

● **Particular traffic regulations:**
Maximum speed for cars:
130 km/h recommended on motorways
90 km/h outside town centres
50 km/h in town centres
Give way: all traffic from the right has right of way, including slow
vehicles, except for major roads and other regulating traffic signs. At
roundabouts the traffic already on the roundabout has priority.
Seat belts: compulsory in the front and the back

 .6 The petrol station

● **The petrol prices in Germany**, Austria and Switzerland are
comparable to those in the UK.

How many kilometres to ___ the next petrol station, please?	Wieviel Kilometer sind es bis zur nächsten Tankstelle?
	veefeel kilomayter zint ez biss tsoor nexten tankshteller?
I would like...litres of..., ___ please	Ich möchte ... Liter
	ikh moekhter ... liter
– super _____	Ich möchte ... Liter Super(benzin)
	ikh moehkter ... liter zooper(bentseen)
– leaded _____	Ich möchte ... Liter normal(es Bezin)
	ikh moekhter ... liter normarl(ez bentseen)
– unleaded_____	Ich möchte ... Liter bleifrei(es Benzin)
	ikh moekhter ... liter blaifrai(ez bentseen)
– diesel _____	Ich möchte ... Liter Diesel
	ikh moekhter ... liter deezel
I would like... _____ Marks/Schilling/ Franks worth of petrol, please	Ich möchte für ... Mark/Schilling/Franken (Auto)gas
	ikh moekhter fuer ... mark/shilling/franken (owto)gass
Fill her up, please _____	Voll bitte
	foll bitter
Could you check...?_____	Würden Sie bitte...kontrollieren?
	vuerden zee bitter...kontrolleeren?
– the oil level _____	Kontrollieren Sie bitte den Ölstand
	kontrolleeren zee bitter dayn oelshtant
– the tyre pressure _____	Kontrollieren Sie bitte den Reifendruck
	kontrolleeren zee bitter dayn raifendrukk
Could you change the ___ oil, please?	Wechseln Sie bitte das Öl
	vekhseln zee bitter dass oel
Could you clean the _____ windows/the windscreen, please?	Reinigen Sie bitte die Windschutzscheibe
	rainigen zee bitter dee vint shoots shaiber
Could you give the car____ a wash, please?	Kann ich hier mein Auto waschen lassen?
	kann ikh main owto heer vashen lassen?

On the road

The parts of a car

(the diagram shows the numbered parts)

1	battery	der Akku/die Batterie	*dayr akoo/batteree*
2	rear light	das Rücklicht	*dass ruekleekht*
3	rear-view mirror	der Rückspiegel	*dayr ruekshpeegell*
	reversing light	der Rückfahrscheinwerfer	*dayr rueckfahrshaynverfer*
4	aerial	die Antenne	*dee antennar*
	car radio	das Autoradio	*dass owtorardiyoo*
5	petrol tank	der Benzintank	*dayr bentseentank*
	inside mirror	der Innenspiegel	*dayr innenshpeegel*
6	sparking plugs	die Zündkerze(n)	*dee tsuentkairtsen*
	fuel filter/pump	das Treibstofffilter/die Triebstoffpumpe	*dass traipshtofffilter/dee traipshtoffpoomper*
7	wing mirror	der Aussenspiegel	*dayr owsenshpeegel*
8	bumper	die Stoßstange	*dee shtoass shtanger*
	carburettor	der Vergaser	*dayr fairgarzer*
	crankcase	das Kurbelgehäuse	*dass koorbellgehoyzer*
	cylinder	der Zylinder	*dayr tsilinder*
	ignition	die Zündung	*dee tsuendoong*
	warning light	die Kontrollampe	*dee kontroal lamper*
	dynamo	der Dynamo	*dayr deenamo*
	accelerator	das Gaspedal	*dass gas pedarl*
	handbrake	die Handbremse	*dee hantbremzer*
	valve	das Ventil	*dass venteel*
9	silencer	der Auspufftopf	*dayr owspufftopf*
10	boot	der Kofferraum	*dayr kofferrowm*
11	headlight	der Scheinwerfer	*dayr shaynverfer*
	crank shaft	die Kurbelwelle	*dee koorbelveller*
12	air filter	das Luftfilter	*dass looftfilter*
	fog lamp	die Nebelleuchte	*dee naybel loykhter*
13	engine block	der Motorblock	*dayr moatorblock*
	camshaft	die Nockenwelle	*dee nokkenveller*
	oil filter/pump	das Ölfilter/dieÖlpumpe	*dass oelfilter/dee oelpoomper*
	dipstick	der Ölstandstab	*dayr oelshtuntshtarp*
	pedal	das Pedal	*dass pedarl*
14	door	die Wagentür	*dee vargentuer*
15	radiator	der Kühler	*dayr kuehler*
16	brake disc	die Bremsscheibe	*dee bremzshayber*
	spare wheel	das Ersatzrad	*dass erzatsrart*
17	indicator	der Blinker	*dayr blinker*
18	windscreen wiper	der Scheibenwischer	*dayr shaibenvisher*
19	shock absorbers	der Stossdämpfer	*dayr shtossdempfer*
	sunroof	das Schiebdach	*dass sheebedakh*
	spoiler	der Spoiler	*dayr shpoyler*
	starter motor	der Startmotor	*dayr shtartmoator*
20	steering column	die Lenksäule	*dee lenkzoyler*
21	exhaust pipe	das Auspuffrohr	*dass owspoofrohr*
22	seat belt	der Sicherheitsgurt	*dayr zikherhaitsgoort*
	fan	der Ventilator	*dayr venteelator*
23	distributor cables	das Verteilerkabel	*dass fertailerkarbel*
24	gear lever	der Schalthebel	*dayr shalt-haybel*

25	windscreen	die Windschutzscheibe	dee vintshootsshaiber
	water pump	die Wasserpumpe	dee vasserpoomper
26	wheel	das Rad	dass rart
27	hubcap	die Radkappe	dee rartkapper
	piston	der Kolben	dayr kolben

On the road

I'm having car trouble. Could you give me a hand?	Ich habe eine Panne. Können Sie mir helfen? *ikh harber ainer panner. koennen zee meer helfen?*
I've run out of petrol	Ich habe kein Benzin mehr *ikh harber kain bentseen mayr*
I've locked the keys in the car	Ich habe die Schlüssel im Auto steckenlassen *ikh harber dee shluessel im owto shtekken lassen*
The car/motorbike/ moped won't start	Das Auto/Motorrad/Moped springt nicht an *dass owto/moator rat/moapet shprinkt nikht an*
Could you contact the recovery service for me, please?	Könnten Sie für mich die Pannenhilfe benachrichtigen? *koennten zee fuer mikh dee pannen hilfer benakh rikhtigen?*
Could you call a garage for me, please?	Könnten Sie für mich eine Werkstatt anrufen? *koennten zee fuer mikh ainer vairkshtatt anroofen?*
Could you give me a lift to...?	Darf ich mit Ihnen nach...mitfahren? *darf ikh mit eenen nakh...mitfahren?*
– a garage/into town?	Darf ich mit Ihnen bis zu einer Werkstatt/in die Stadt mitfahren? *darf ikh mit eenen biss tsoo ainer verkshtatt/in dee shtatt mit fahren?*
– a phone booth?	Darf ich mit Ihnen bis zu einer Telefonzelle mitfahren? *darf ikh mit eenen biss tsoo ainer tellefoan tseller mit fahren?*
– an emergency phone?	Darf ich mit Ihnen bis zu einer Rufsäule mitfahren? *darf ikh mit eenen biss tsoo ainer roofzoyler mit fahren?*
Can we take my bicycle/moped?	Kann mein Fahrrad/Moped auch mit? *kann main fahr rat/moapet owkh mit?*
Could you tow me to a garage?	Könnten Sie mich zu einer Werkstatt (ab)schleppen? *koennten zee mikh tsoo ainer verkshtatt (ap)shleppen?*
There's probably something wrong with...(See pages 51–52)	Wahrscheinlich ist mit dem/der/ den...etwas nicht in Ordnung *varshainlikh ist mit daym/dayr/dayn...etvass nikht in ordnoong*
Can you fix it?	Können Sie es reparieren? *koennen zee es repareeren?*
Could you fix my tyre?	Können Sie den Reifen flicken? *koennen zee dayn raifen flikken?*
Could you change this wheel?	Können Sie das Rad wechseln? *koennen zee dass rart vekhzeln?*

Can you fix it so it'll get me to...?	Können Sie es soweit reparieren, dass ich damit nach ... fahren kann?
	koennen zee es zovait repareeren dass ikh darmit nakh ... fahren kann?
Which garage can help me?	Welche Werkstatt kann mir denn dann helfen?
	velkher verkshtatt kann meer denn dann helfen?
When will my car/bicycle be ready?	Wann ist mein Auto/Fahrrad fertig?
	vann ist main owto/fahr rart fairtikh?
Can I wait for it here?	Kann ich hier darauf warten?
	kann ikh heer darrowf varten?
How much will it cost?	Wieviel wird es kosten?
	veefeel virt es kosten?
Could you itemise the bill?	Können Sie die Rechnung spezifizieren?
	koennen zee dee rekhnoong shpetsi fitseeren?
Can I have a receipt for the insurance?	Ich hätte gern eine Quittung für die Versicherung
	ikh hetter gayrn ainer kvittoong fuer dee fairzikheroong

.8 The bicycle/moped

See the diagram on page 55.

● **Cycle paths** are common in towns and cities and their use is strongly recommended. Bikes can usually be hired at tourist centres. The maximum speed for mopeds is 40 km/h both inside and outside town centres. Crash helmets are compulsory.

Ich habe keine Ersatzteile für Ihren Wagen/Ihr Fahrrad	I don't have parts for your car/bicycle
Ich muss die Ersatzteile irgendwo anders besorgen	I have to get the parts from somewhere else
Ich muss die Ersatzteile bestellen	I have to order the parts
Das dauert einen halben Tag	That'll take half a day
Das dauert einen Tag	That'll take a day
Das dauert ein paar Tage	That'll take a few days
Das dauert eine Woche	That'll take a week
Ihr Auto ist schrottreif	Your car is a write-off
Hier ist nichts mehr zu machen	It can't be repaired
Das Auto/Motorrad/Moped/Fahrrad ist um...Uhr fertig	The car/motor bike/moped/bicycle will be ready at...o'clock

The parts of a bicycle
(the diagram shows the numbered parts)

1	rear lamp	das Rücklicht	*dass rueklikht*
2	rear wheel	das Hinterrad	*dass hinterrart*
3	(luggage) carrier	der Gepäckträger	*dayr gepektrayger*
4	bicycle fork	das Steuer(kopf)rohr	*dass shtoyerkopfrohr*
5	bell	die Klingel	*dee klingel*
	inner tube	der Schlauch	*dayr shlowkh*
	tyre	der Reifen	*dayr raifen*
6	crank	die Kurbel	*dee koorbel*
7	gear change	der Umwerfer	*dayr oomverfer*
	wire	das Kabel	*dass karbel*
	dynamo	der Dynamo	*dayr deenamo*
	bicycle trailer	der Fahrradanhänger	*dayr fahrrartanhenger*
	frame	der Rahmen	*dayr rarmen*
8	dress guard	der Kleiderschutz	*dayr klaidershoots*
9	chain	die Kette	*dee ketter*
	chain guard	der Kettenschutz	*dayr kettenshoots*
	chain lock	das Kettenschloss	*dass kettenshloss*
	milometer	der Kilometerzähler	*dayr keelomaytertsayler*
	child's seat	der Kindersitz	*dayr kinderzits*
10	headlamp	der Scheinwerfer	*dayr shainverfer*
	bulb	die Birne	*dee beerner*
11	pedal	das Pedal	*dass pedarl*
12	pump	die Pumpe	*dee poomper*
13	reflector	der Rückstrahler	*dayr ruekshtrarler*
14	break pad	die Bremsbacke	*dee bremzbakker*
15	brake cable	das Bremskabel	*dass bremzkarbel*
16	ring lock	das Sicherheitsschloss	*dass zikherhaitsshloss*
17	carrier straps	das Spannband	*dass shpannbant*
	tachometer	der Tacho(meter)	*dayr takhomayter*
18	spoke	die Speiche	*die shpaikher*
19	mudguard	das Schutzblech	*dass shootsblekh*
20	handlebar	der Lenker	*dayr lenker*
21	chain wheel	das Zahnrad	*dass tsarnrart*
	toe clip	der Rennhaken	*dayr renharken*
22	crank axle	die Tretwelle	*dee traytveller*
	drum brake	die Trommelbremse	*dee trommelbremzer*
	rim	die Felge	*dee felger*
23	valve	das Ventil	*dass venteel*
24	valve tube	der Ventilschlauch	*dayr venteelshlowkh*
25	gear cable	das Gangschaltungskabel	*dass gangshaltoongskarbel*
26	fork	die Vorderradgabel	*dee forderrartgarbel*
27	front wheel	das Vorderrad	*dass forderrart*
28	seat	der Sattel	*dayr zattel*

🔵.9 Renting a vehicle

I'd like to rent a..._____	Ich möchte ein(en)...mieten
	ikh moekhter ain(en)...meeten
Do I need a (special)_____ licence for that?	Brauche ich dafür einen (bestimmten) Führerschein?
	browkher ikh dafuer ainen (beshtimmten) fuehrershain?
I'd like to rent the...for... __	Ich möchte den/das...für...mieten
	ikh moekhter dayn/dass...fuer...meeten
– one day_____	Ich möchte den/das...für einen Tag mieten
	ikh moekhter dayn/dass...fuer ainen tark meeten
– two days _____	Ich möchte den/da ...für zwei Tage mieten
	ikh moekhter dayn/dass...fuer tsvai targer meeten
How much is that per_____ day/week?	Wieviel kostet das pro Tag/Woche?
	veefeel kostet dass pro tark/vokher?
How much is the _____ deposit?	Wie hoch ist die Kaution?
	vee hokh ist dee kowtseeoan?
Could I have a receipt _____ for the deposit?	Geben Sie mir bitte eine Quittung, dass ich die Kaution bezahlt habe
	gayben zee meer bitter ainer kvittoong, dass ikh dee kowtseeoan betsarlt harber
How much is the _____ surcharge per kilometre?	Wie hoch ist der zusätzliche Kilometerpreis?
	vee hokh ist dayr tsoo zetslikher kilo mayter praiss?
Does that include petrol? __	Ist das Benzin mit enthalten?
	ist dass bentseen mit enthalten?
Does that include _____ insurance?	Ist die Versicherung mit enthalten?
	ist dee fairsikhe roong mit enthalten?
What time can I pick_____ the...up tomorrow?	Wann kann ich das...morgen abholen?
	vann kann ikh dass...morgen apholen?
When does the...have _____ to be back?	Wann muss ich den/das...zurückbringen?
	vann mooss ikh dayn/dass...tsooruekbringen?
Where's the petrol tank? __	Wo ist der Tank?
	vo ist dayr tank?
What sort of fuel does _____ it take?	Was muss ich tanken?
	vass mooss ikh tanken?

🔵.10 Hitchhiking

Where are you heading?___	Wohin fahren Sie?
	vohin fahren zee?
Can I come along? _____	Darf ich mit Ihnen mitfahren?
	darf ikh mit eenen mit fahren?
Can my boyfriend/ _____ girlfriend come too?	Darf mein Freund/meine Freundin auch mit?
	darf main froynt/mainer froyndin owkh mitt?
I'm trying to get to..._____	Ich muss nach ...
	ikh mooss nakh ...
Is that on the way to...? ___	Liegt das auf dem Weg nach...
	leekt dass owf daym vayk nakh...

Could you drop me off...?	Könnten Sie mich absetzen?
	koennten zee mikh apsetsen?
– here?	Könnten Sie mich hier absetzen?
	koennten zee mikh heer apsetsen?
– at the...exit?	Könnten Sie mich an der Ausfahrt nach... absetzen?
	koennten zee mikh an dayr owsfahrt nakh... apsetsen?
– in the centre?	Könnten Sie mich im Zentrum absetzen?
	koennten zee mikh im tsentroom apsetsen?
– at the next roundabout?	Könnten Sie mich beim nächsten Kreisel/Kreisverkehr absetzen?
	koennten zee mikh baim nexten kraizel/krais fair kayr apzetsen?
Could you stop here, please?	Würden Sie bitte hier halten?
	vuerden zee bitter heer halten?
I'd like to get out here	Ich möchte hier raus
	ikh moekhter heer rows
Thanks for the lift	Vielen Dank fürs Mitnehmen
	feelen dunk fuers mitnaymen

Public transport

6 **P**ublic transport

6.1 **I**n general

● **Public transport** in Germany prides itself for being on time. Strikes (*Streiks*) are rare and only tend to occur around the trade unions' negotiations on pay which take place once a year. Tickets for buses can be bought as you get on the bus. Some unlimited travel cards/runabout tickets purchased for use on trains also cover all public means of transport within a designated area (*Verkehrsverbund*). Train tickets can be purchased either at the ticket office in the station or at ticket machines on the platforms.

Announcements

Der Zug nach...von...hat _____ eine Verspätung von...Minuten.	The train to...from has been delayed by...minutes.
Auf Gleis ... fährt ein der Zug _____ nach.../aus...	The train now arriving at platform...is the train to.../from...
Auf Gleis...steht der Zug zur Abfahrt ____ bereit nach...	The train to...is about to leave from platform...
Achtung! Bitte zurückbleiben! _____ Ein Intercity fährt durch auf Gleis...	Attention please, keep your distance from the rail track, an intercity train will pass on platform...
Wir nähern uns (der Station/dem _____ Hauptbahnhof)...	We're now approaching...(the station/ main station)

Where does this train_____ go to?	Wohin fährt dieser Zug? *vohinn fairt deezer tsook?*
Does this boat go to...? ____	Fährt dieses Schiff nach ...? *fairt deezes shiff nakh...?*
Can I take this bus to...? ____	Kann ich mit diesem Bus nach...fahren? *kann ikh mitt deezem boos nakh...fahren?*
Does this train stop at...? __	Hält dieser Zug in...? *helt deezer tsook in...?*
Is this seat taken/free/ _____ reserved?	Ist dieser Platz besetzt/frei/reserviert? *ist deezer plats bezetst/frai/rezerveert?*
I've booked... _____	Ich habe ... reservieren lassen *ikh haber ... rezerveeren lassen*
Could you tell me _____ where I have to get off for... ?	Könnten Sie mir sagen, wo ich aussteigen muss, um zu/zum/zur/zu den ... zu kommen? *koennten zee meer zargen, vo ikh ows shtaigen mooss, oom tsoo/tsoom/tsoor/tsoo dayn ... tsoo kommen?*
Could you let me_____ know when we get to...?	Würden Sie mir bitte Bescheid sagen, wenn wir bei/beim/bei der/bei den ... sind? *vuerden zee meer bitter beshait zargen, venn veer bai/baim/bai dayr/bai dayn ... zint?*

Could you stop at the _____ next stop, please?	Halten Sie bitte an der nächsten Haltestelle
	halten zee bitter an dayr nexten halter shteller
Where are we now? _____	Wo sind wir hier?
	vo zint veer heer?
Do I have to get off here? __	Muss ich hier aussteigen?
	mooss ikh heer ows shtaigen?
Have we already _____ passed...?	Sind wir schon an/am/an der ... vorbei?
	zint veer shoan an/am/an dayr ... forbai?
How long have I been _____ asleep?	Wie lange habe ich geschlafen?
	vee langer harber ikh geshlarfen?
How long does... _____ stop here?	Wie lange bleibt der/die ... hier stehen?
	vee langer blaipt dayr/dee ... heer shtayhen?
Can I come back on the ____ same ticket?	Kann ich mit dieser Fahrkarte auch wieder zurück?
	kann ikh mit deezer farkarter owkh veeder tsooruek?
Can I change on this_____ ticket?	Kann ich mit dieser Fahrkarte umsteigen?
	kann ikh mit deezer farkarter oom shtaigen?
How long is this ticket ____ valid for?	Wie lange ist diese Fahrkarte gültig?
	vee langer ist deezer farkarter gueltikh?
How much is the _____ supplement for the intercity?	Wie hoch ist der IC Zuschlag?
	vee hokh ist der ee tsee tsooschlark?

6.2 Questions to passengers

Ticket types

Erster oder zweiter Klasse? _____	First or second class?
Einfach oder hin und zurück/Hin- und ___ Rückfahrt?	Single or return?
Raucher oder Nichtraucher? _____	Smoking or non-smoking?
Am Fenster oder am Gang? _____	Window or aisle?
Vorn oder hinten? _____	Front or back?
Sitzplatz oder Liegewagen? _____	Seat or couchette?
Oben, in der Mitte oder unten? _____	Top, middle or bottom?
Touristenklasse oder Business Class?____	Tourist class or business class?
Kabine oder Sitzplatz? _____	Cabin or seat?
Einzel- oder Doppelkabine? _____	Single or double?
Zu wieviel Personen reisen Sie? _____	How many are travelling?

Destination

Wohin reisen Sie? _____	Where are you travelling?
Wann reisen Sie ab? _____	When are you leaving?
Abfahrt/(aircraft) Abflug um..._____	Your...leaves at...
Sie müssen in...umsteigen_____	You have to change trains at...
Sie müssen in...aussteigen _____	You have to get off at...
Sie müssen über...reisen _____	You have to travel via...
Die Hinreise fängt am...an _____	The outward journey is on...
Die Rückreise beginnt am..._____	The return journey is on...
Sie müssen spätestens...an Bord sein __	You have to be on board by...

Inside the vehicle

Ihre Fahrkarte bitte_____	Your ticket, please
Ihre Reservierung bitte _____	Your reservation, please
Ihren (Reise)pass bitte_____	Your passport, please
Sie sitzen auf dem falschen Platz_____	You're in the wrong seat
Sie sitzen im/in der falschen... _____	You're on/in the wrong...
Dieser Platz ist reserviert _____	This seat is reserved
Sie müssen einen Zuschlag (be)zahlen __	You'll have to pay a supplement
Der/die/das...hat eine Verspätung von __ ...Minuten	The...has been delayed by...minutes

6.3 Tickets

Where can I...? _____	Wo kann ich...?
	vo kann ikh...?
– buy a ticket?_____	Wo kann ich eine Karte kaufen?
	vo kann ikh ainer karter kowfen?
– make a reservation? _____	Wo kann ich einen Platz reservieren lassen?
	vo kann ikh ainen plats rezerveeren lassen?
– book a flight?_____	Wo kann ich einen Flug buchen?
	vo kann ikh ainen flook bookhen?
Could I have a...to..., please?	Ich möchte...nach...
	ikh moekhter...nakh...
– a single _____	Ich möchte einmal einfach nach...
	ikh moekhter ainmarl ainfakh nakh...
– a return _____	Ich möchte eine Rückfahrkarte nach...
	ikh moekhter ainer ruekfarkarter nakh...
first class _____	erster Klasse
	airster klasser
second class _____	zweiter Klasse
	tsvaiter klasser
tourist class_____	Touristenklasse
	tooristen klasser

business class	Business Class
	bizniss klarss
I'd like to book a seat/couchette/cabin	Ich möchte einen Sitzplatz/Liegewagenplatz/eine Kabine reservieren lassen
	ikh moekhter ainen zits plats/leeger vargen plats/ainer kabiner rezerveeren lassen
I'd like to book a berth in the sleeping car	Ich möchte einen Platz im Schlafwagen reservieren lassen
	ikh moekhter ainen plats im shlarfvargen rezerveeren lassen
top/middle/bottom	oben/in der Mitte/unten
	oaben/in dayr mitter/oonten
smoking/no smoking	Raucher/Nichtraucher
	rowkher/nikht rowkher
by the window	am Fenster
	am fenster
single/double	Einzel-/Doppel-
	aintsel-/doppel-
at the front/back	vorn/hinten
	forn/hinten
There are...of us	Wir sind zu ...t (e.g. zweit, dritt, viert)
	veer zint tsoo ...t (e.g. tsvait, dritt, feert)
a car	ein Auto
	ain owto
a caravan	ein Wohnwagen
	ain voanvargen
...bicycles	...Fahrräder
	...fahr rayder
Do you also have...?	Haben Sie...?
	harben zee...?
– season tickets?	Haben Sie Sammelfahrscheine?
	harben zee zammel fahr shainer?
– weekly tickets?	Haben Sie Wochenkarten?
	harben zee vokhen karten?
– monthly season tickets?	Haben Sie Monatskarten?
	harben zee moanarts karten?
Where's?	Wo ist...?

6.4 Information

	Wo ist...?
	vo ist...?
Where's the information desk?	Wo ist die Auskunft?
	vo ist dee owskoonft?
Where can I find a timetable?	Wo ist die Tafel mit den Abfahrtszeiten/Ankunftszeiten?
	vo ist dee tarfel mit den apfahrtstsaiten/ankunftstsaiten?
Where's the...desk?	Wo ist der Schalter für...?
	vo ist dayr shalter fuer...?
Do you have a city map with the bus/the underground routes on it?	Haben Sie einen Stadtplan mit dem Bus-/U-Bahnnetz?
	harben zee ainen shtatplarn mit dem booss-/oobarn nets?
Do you have a timetable?	Haben Sie einen Fahrplan?
	harben zee ainen farplarn?

I'd like to confirm/cancel/change my booking for/trip to...	Ich möchte meine Reservierung/Reise nach...bestätigen/annullieren/ändern *ikh moekhter mainer rezerveerung/raizer nakh ... beshtaytigen/annoo leeren/endern*
Will I get my money back?	Bekomme ich mein Geld zurück? *bekommer ikh main gelt tsooruek?*
I want to go to... How do I get there? (What's the quickest way there?)	Ich muss nach... Wie komme ich da (am schnellsten) hin? *ikh mooss nakh... vee kommer ikh da (am shnellsten) hin?*
How much is a single/return to...?	Wieviel kostet eine Fahrt/Rückfahrkarte nach...? *veefeel kostet ainer fart/ruek fahr karter nakh...?*
Do I have to pay a supplement?	Muss ich Zuschlag zahlen? *mooss ikh tsooshlak tsarlen?*
Can I interrupt my journey with this ticket?	Darf ich die Reise mit diesem Ticket unterbrechen? *darf ikh dee raizer mit deezem ticket oonter brekhen?*
How much luggage am I allowed?	Wieviel Gepäck darf ich mitnehmen? *veefeel gepeck darf ikh mitnaymen?*
Does this...travel direct?	Geht diese(r)/dieses ... direkt? *gayt deeze(r)/deezes ... direkt?*
Do I have to change? Where?	Muss ich umsteigen? Wo? *mooss ikh oom shtaigen? vo?*
Will there be any stopovers?	Macht das Flugzeug eine Zwischenlandung? *makht dass flooktsoyk ainer tsvishen landoong?*
Does the boat call in at any ports on the way?	Legt das Schiff unterwegs in irgendwelchen Häfen an? *laykt dass shiff oontervegz in eergent velkhen hayfen an?*
Does the train/bus stop at...?	Hält der Zug/Bus in...? *helt der tsook/booss in...?*
Where should I get off?	Wo muss ich aussteigen? *vo mooss ikh ows shtaigen?*
Is there a connection to...?	Gibt es einen Anschluss nach...? *gipt ez ainen anschluss nakh...?*
How long do I have to wait?	Wie lange muss ich warten? *vee langer mooss ikh varten?*
When does...leave?	Wann fährt...ab? *vann fairt...ap?*
What time does the first/next/last...leave?	Wann fährt/(aircraft) fliegt der/die/das erste/nächste/letzte...? *vann fairt/fleekt dayr/dee/dass airster/nexter/letster...?*
How long does...take?	Wie lange dauert die Fahrt/(flight) der Flug? *vee langer dowert dee fahrt/dayr flook?*
What time does...arrive in...?	Wann kommt...in...an? *vann kommt...in...an?*
Where does the...to... leave from?	Wo fährt/(aircraft) fliegt der/die/das nach ...ab? *vo fairt/fleekt dayr/dee/duss nakh...ap?*
Is this...to...?	Ist dies ... nach...? *ist deez ... nakh...?*

.5 Aeroplanes

● **On arrival** at a German airport (Flughafen), you will find the
following signs:

Abflug	domestic/international	Ankunft
Inland/Ausland	departures	arrivals

After the check-in a boarding pass (Bordkarte, Einsteigekarte) is handed
out which details the gate (Flugsteig) and departure time (Abflugzeit).

.6 Trains

● **The rail network** is extensive. The Deutsche Bundesbahn is
responsible for the national rail traffic. Generally there are four types of
trains: *Intercity*, *Eilzug/Schnellzug* (fast train which does not stop at
small stations - long distance), *S-Bahn* (designed to link smaller towns
and villages on the outskirts with the city centre), *U-Bahn*
(underground). A supplement is only to be paid for the *Intercity*. Seats
can be reserved in advance on the *Intercity* and *Eilzug* only.

.7 Taxis

● **In nearly all** large cities and bigger towns, there are plenty of taxis.
Although German taxis have no fixed colour, they tend to be cream
coloured. Virtually all taxis have a meter.

Besetzt	Frei	Taxistand
booked	for hire	taxi rank

Taxi! _____	Taxi!
	tarksi!
Could you get me a taxi, ___ please?	Würden Sie mir bitte ein Taxi/eine Taxe bestellen?
	vuerden zee meer bitter ain tarksi/ainer tarkser beshtellen?
Where can I find a taxi_____ around here?	Wo finde ich hier in der Nähe ein Taxi?
	vo finder ikh heer in dayr nayher ain tarksi?
Could you take me to..., ___ please?	Zu/zum/zur ... bitte
	tsoo/tsoom/tsoor ... bitter
– this address _____	Zu dieser Adresse bitte
	tsoo deezer adresser bitter
– the...hotel _____	Zum Hotel ... bitte
	tsoom hotel ... bitter
– the town/city centre_____	Ins Zentrum bitte
	ins tsentroom bitter
– the station _____	Zum Bahnhof bitte
	tsoom barnhoaf bitter
– the airport _____	Zum Flughafen bitte
	tsoom flook harfen bitter
How much is the _____ trip to...?	Wieviel kostet die Fahrt zu/zum/zur...?
	veefeel kostet dee fart tsoo/tsoom/tsoor...?

Public transport

English	German
How far is it to...? _____	Wie weit ist es nach ...?
	vee vait ist ez nakh ...?
Could you turn on the _____ meter, please?	Würden Sie bitte das Taxameter einschalten?
	vuerden zee bitter dass taksarmeter ainshalten?
I'm in a hurry _____	Ich habe es eilig
	ikh haber ez ailikh
Could you speed _____ up/slow down a little?	Könnten Sie etwas schneller/langsamer fahren?
	koennten zee etvass shneller/langzarmer fahren?
Could you take a _____ different route?	Könnten Sie eine andere Strecke fahren?
	koennten zee ainer anderer shtrekker fahren?
I'd like to get out here,_____ please.	Lassen Sie mich hier aussteigen
	lassen zee mikh heer owsshtaigen
You have to go...here _____	Sie müssen gehen...
	zee muessen gayhen...
You have to go straight on here.	hier geradeaus
	heer gerarder ows
You have to turn left_____ here	hier (nach) links
	heer (nakh) links
You have to turn right _____ here.	hier (nach) rechts
	heer (nakh) rekhts
This is it _____	Hier ist es
	heer ist ez
Could you wait a minute___ for me, please?	Warten Sie bitte einen Augenblick
	varten zee bitter ainen owgenblick

Public transport

Overnight accommodation

7 Overnight accommodation

7.1 General

● **There is a great variety** in overnight accommodation in Germany.
Hotels: the 'star-system' does not tend to be operational in Germany.
However, some are hotels '*vom ADAC empfohlen*' (recommended by
the German motoring organisation) promising good standard. Most
hotels offer *Halbpension* (half board) or *Vollpension* (full board).
Pension/Gasthof/Gästehaus: often smaller houses with B + B type
accommodation. A *Gasthof* would also have a restaurant.
Rasthof: accommodation available at motorway service stations.
Ferienwohnungen: holiday flats available in many tourist places,
recreational centres and/or camping sites.
Berghütten: mountain hut providing basic sleeping space.
Jugendherberge: Youth Hostels in Germany require an international
Youth Hostel pass and usually expect clients to provide their own linen.
Campingplatz: free camping is not allowed in Germany. Camping sites
are usually privately run and not open all year round.

Wie lange bleiben Sie?	How long will you be staying?
Würden Sie bitte das Formular ausfüllen?	Fill out this form, please
Dürfte ich bitte Ihren Pass haben?	Could I see your passport?
Sie müssen eine Kaution stellen/zahlen	I'll need a deposit
Sie müssen im voraus (be)zahlen	You'll have to pay in advance

My name's...I've made a reservation over the phone/by mail	Mein Name ist...Ich habe einen Platz reservieren lassen (telefonisch/schriftlich) *main narmer ist...ikh harber ainen plats rezerveeren lassen (telefoanish/shriftlikh)*
How much is it per night/week/ month?	Wieviel kostet es pro Nacht/Woche/Monat? *veefeel kostet ez pro nakht/vokher/moanart?*
We'll be staying at least...nights/weeks	Wir bleiben mindestens...Nächte/Wochen *veer blaiben mindestens...nekhter/vokhen*
We don't know yet	Das wissen wir noch nicht genau *dass vissen veer nokh nikht genow*
Do you allow pets (cats/dogs)?	Sind Haustiere (Hunde/Katzen) erlaubt? *zint howzteerer (hunder/katsen) erlowpt?*
What time does the gate/door open/close?	Wann ist die Pforte/Tür geöffnet/(auf)/geschlossen/(zu)? *van ist dee pforter/tuer geoeffnet/(owf)/geshlossen/(tsoo)?*
Could you get me a taxi, please?	Würden Sie mir bitte ein Taxi bestellen? *vuerden zee meer bitter ain tarksi beshtellen?*
Is there any mail for me?	Ist Post für mich da? *ist posst fuer mikh dar?*

Camping equipment
(the diagram shows the numbered parts)

luggage space	das Gepäckapsis	*dass gepekapsis*
can opener	der Dosenöffner	*dayr doazenoefner*
butane gas bottle	die Butangasflasche	*dee bootarn gasflasher*
1 pannier	die Packtasche	*dee pakktasher*
2 gas cooker	der Gaskocher	*dayr gasskokher*
3 groundsheet	die Bodenplane	*dee boadenplarner*
mallet	der Hammer	*dayr hammer*
hammock	die Hängematte	*dee hengermatter*
4 jerry can	der Kanister	*dayr kannister*
campfire	das Lagerfeuer	*dass largerfoyer*
5 folding chair	der Klappstuhl	*dayr klapshtool*
6 insulated picnic box	die Kühltasche	*dee kuehltasher*
ice pack	das Kühlelement	*dass kuehlelement*
compass	der Kompass	*dayr kompas*
wick	der Glühstrumpf	*dayr gluehshtroompf*
corkscrew	der Korkenzieher	*dayr korkentseeyer*
7 airbed	die Luftmatratze	*dee looftmatrattser*
8 airbed plug pump	der Matratzenstöpsel	*dayr matrattsenshtoepsel*
9 awning	das Vordach	*dass fordakh*
10 karimat	die Matte	*dee matter*
11 pan	die Pfanne	*dee pfanner*
12 pan handle	der Pfannenstiel	*dayr pfannenshteel*
primus stove	der Petroleumkocher	*dayr petroaleyoomkokher*
zip	der Reissverschluss	*dayr raissfershluss*
13 backpack	der Rucksack	*dayr rookzakk*
14 guy rope	die Zeltleine	*dee tseltlainer*
sleeping bag	der Schlafsack	*dayr shlarfzak*
15 storm lantern	die Sturmlaterne	*dee shtoormlaterner*
camp bed	die Liege	*leeger*
table	der Tisch	*dayr tish*
16 tent	das Zelt	*dass tselt*
17 tent peg	der Hering	*dayr hayring*
18 tent pole	die Zeltstange	*dee tseltshtanger*
vacuum flask	die Thermosflasche	*dee termowsflasher*
19 water bottle	die Feldflasche	*dee feltflasher*
clothes peg	die Wäscheklammer	*dee vesherklummer*
clothes line	die Wäscheleine	*dee vesherlainer*
windbreak	der Windschutz	*dayr vintshoots*
20 torch	die Taschenlampe	*dee tashenlamper*
pocket knife	das Taschenmesser	*dass tashenmesser*

Overnight accommodation

See the diagram on page 69.

Sie können sich selbst einen Platz aussuchen	You can pick your own site
Sie bekommen einen Platz zugewiesen	You'll be allocated a site
Dies ist Ihre Platznummer	This is your site number.
Kleben Sie dies bitte auf Ihr Auto	Stick this on your car, please.
Sie dürfen diese Karte nicht verlieren	Please don't lose this card

Where's the manager?	Wo ist der Verwalter?
	vo ist der fairvalter?
Are we allowed to camp here?	Dürfen wir hier campen?
	duerfen veer heer kampen?
There are...of us and ...tents	Wir sind ... Personen und haben ... Zelte
	veer zint ... perzoanen oont harben ... tselter
Can we pick our own site?	Dürfen wir selbst einen Platz aussuchen?
	duerfen veer zelpst ainen plats ows zookhen?
Do you have a quiet spot for us?	Haben Sie einen ruhigen Platz für uns?
	harben zee ainen roohigen plats fuer oons?
Do you have any other sites available?	Haben Sie keinen anderen freien Platz?
	harben zee kainen anderen fraien plats?
It's too windy/sunny/ shady here.	Hier ist zuviel Wind/Sonne/Schatten
	heer ist tsoofeel vint/zonner/shatten
It's too crowded here	Hier ist es zu voll
	heer ist es tsoo foll
The ground's too hard/uneven	Der Boden ist zu hart/ungleichmässig
	der boaden ist tsoo hart/oon glaikh mayssikh
Do you have a level spot for the camper/caravan/folding caravan?	Haben Sie einen horizontalen Platz für das Wohnmobil/den Wohnwagen/Faltwagen?
	harben zee ainen horitsontarlen plats fuer dass voan moabeel/dayn voanvargen/faltvargen?
Could we have adjoining sites?	Können wir beieinander stehen?
	koennen veer baiainander shtayhen?
Can we park the car next to the tent?	Darf das Auto beim Zelt geparkt werden?
	darf dass owto baim tselt geparkt verden?
How much is it per person/tent/caravan/car?	Was kostet es pro Person/Zelt/Wohnwagen/Auto?
	vass kostet ez pro perzoan/tselt/voanvargen/owto?
Are there any...?	Gibt es...?
	gipt ez...?
– any hot showers?	Warmwasserduschen?
	varm vasser dooshen?
– washing machines?	Waschmaschinen?
	wash masheenen?
Is there a...on the site?	Gibt es auf dem Gelände...?
	gipt ez owf daym gelender...?

Overnight accommodation

Is there a children's ___ play area on the site?	...einen Kinderspielplatz? *...ainen kinder shpeel plats?*
Are there covered ___ cooking facilities on the site?	...eine überdachte Kochgelegenheit? *...ainer ueber dakhter kokh gelaygen hait?*
Can I rent a safe here? ___	Kann ich hier ein Schliessfach mieten? *kann ikh heer ain shleesfakh meeten?*
Are we allowed to ___ barbecue here?	Darf man hier grillen? *darf man heer grillen?*
Are there any power___ points?	Gibt es Elektroanschlüsse? *gipt ez elektro anshluesser?*
	Wann wird der Abfall abgeholt? *vann virt dayr apfal apgeholt?*
When's the rubbish___ collected?	Verkaufen Sie Gasflaschen (Butangas/Propangas)?
Do you sell gas bottles ___ (butane gas/propane gas)?	*fairkowfen zee gassflashen (bootarn gass/proparn gass)?*

🢖 .3 Hotel/B&B/apartment/holiday house

Do you have a ___ single/double room available?	Haben Sie ein Einzelzimmer/Doppelzimmer frei? *harben zee ain aintsel tsimmer/doppel tsimmer frai?*
per person/per room ___	pro Person/pro Zimmer *pro perzoan/pro tsimmer*
Does that include ___ breakfast/lunch/dinner?	Ist das einschliesslich Frühstück/Mittagessen/Abendessen? *ist dass ainshleeslikh frueh shtuek/mittark essen/arbent essen?*
Could we have two___ adjoining rooms?	Können wir zwei Zimmer nebeneinander bekommen? *koennen veer tsvai tsimmer nayben ainander bekommen?*
with/without ___ toilet/bath/shower	Mit/ohne eigener Toilette/eigenem Bad/eigener Dusche *mit/oaner aigener twaletter/aigenem bart/aigener doosher*
(not) facing the street___	(nicht) an der Strassenseite *(nikht) an dayr shtrassen zaiter*
with/without a view ___ of the sea	mit/ohne Seesicht *mit/oaner zayzikht*
Is there...in the hotel?___	Gibt es im Hotel...? *gipt ez im hotel...?*
Is there a lift in the ___ hotel?	Gibt es im Hotel einen Fahrstuhl? *gipt ez im hotel ainen fahrshtool?*
Do you have room ___ service?	Gibt es im Hotel Zimmerservice? *gipt ez im hotel tsimmer zairviss?*
Could I see the room? ___	Könnte ich das Zimmer mal sehen? *koennter ikh dass tsimmer marl zayhen?*
I'll take this room___	Ich nehme dieses Zimmer *ikh naymer deezes tsimmer*
We don't like this one ___	Dieses gefällt uns nicht *deezes gefellt oons nikht*

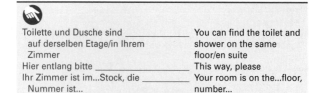

Toilette und Dusche sind _____ auf derselben Etage/in Ihrem Zimmer	You can find the toilet and shower on the same floor/en suite
Hier entlang bitte _____	This way, please
Ihr Zimmer ist im...Stock, die _____ Nummer ist...	Your room is on the...floor, number...

Do you have a larger/_____ less expensive room?	Haben Sie ein grösseres/billigeres Zimmer?
	harben zee ain groesseres/billeegeres tsimmer?
Could you put in a cot? ____	Können Sie ein Kinderbett dazustellen?
	koennen zee ain kinder bet datsoo shtellen?
What time's breakfast? ____	Ab wann gibt es Frühstück?
	ap vann gipt ez frueh shtuek?
Where's the dining _____ room?	Wo ist der Speisesaal?
	vo ist dayr shpaize zarl?
Can I have breakfast_____ in my room?	Kann ich Frühstück aufs Zimmer bekommen?
	kann ikh frueh shtuek owfs tsimmer bekommen?
Where's the emergency____ exit/fire escape?	Wo ist der Notausgang/die Feuertreppe?
	vo ist der noat owsgang/dee foyer trepper?
Where can I park my _____ car (safely)?	Wo kann ich mein Auto (sicher) abstellen?
	vo kann ikh main owto (zikher) apshtellen?
The key to room..., _____ please	Den Schlüssel für Zimmer...bitte
	dayn shluessel fuer tsimmer...bitter
Could you put this in _____ the safe, please?	Darf ich dies bitte in Ihren Safe legen?
	darf ikh dees bitter in eeren safe laygen?
Could you wake me _____ at...tomorrow?	Wecken Sie mich morgen bitte um...Uhr
	vekken zee mikh morgen bitter oom...ooer
Could you find a _____ babysitter for me?	Können Sie mir einen Babysitter besorgen?
	koennen zee meer ainen babysitter bezorgen?
Could I have an extra_____ blanket?	Würden Sie bitte eine extra Decke bringen?
	vuerden zee bitter ainer ekstrar dekker bringen?
What days do the _____ cleaners come in?	An welchen Tagen wird saubergemacht?
	an velkhen targen virt zowber gemakht?
When are the sheets/ _____ towels/tea towels changed?	Wann werden die Bettlaken/Handtücher/Geschirrtücher gewechselt?
	vann verden dee bett larken/hant tuekher/geshirr tuekher gevekhselt?

Overnight accommodation

.4 Complaints

We can't sleep for _____ the noise	Wir können durch den Lärm nicht schlafen
	veer koennen doorkh den lerm nikht shlarfen
Could you turn the _____ radio down, please?	Könnten Sie das Radio bitte etwas leiser stellen?
	koennten zee dass radeeo bitter etvass laizer shtellen?
We're out of toilet paper ___	Das Toilettenpapier ist alle
	dass twaletten papeer ist aller
There aren't any.../ _____ there's not enough...	Es gibt keine.../nicht genug...
	es gipt kainer.../nikht genook ...
The bed linen's dirty_____	Die Bettwäsche ist schmutzig
	dee bettvesher ist shmootsikh
The room hasn't been _____ cleaned.	Das Zimmer ist nicht saubergemacht
	dass tsimmer ist nikht zowber gemakht
The kitchen is not clean____	Die Küche ist nicht sauber
	dee kuekher ist nikht zowber
The kitchen utensils are____ dirty	Die Küchengeräte sind schmutzig
	dee kuekhen gerayter zint shmootsikh
The heater's not_____ working	Die Heizung funktioniert nicht
	dee haitsoong foonk tseeoneert nikht
There's no (hot) _____ water/electricity	Es gibt kein (warmes) Wasser/keinen Strom
	ez gipt kain (varmez) vasser/kainen shtroam
...is broken_____	... ist kaputt
	... ist kapoott
Could you have that _____ seen to?	Können Sie das in Ordnung bringen lassen?
	koennen zee dass in ordnoong bringen lassen?
Could I have another _____ room/site?	Könnte ich ein anderes Zimmer/einen anderen Stellplatz bekommen?
	koennter ikh ain underes tsimmer/ainen anderen stellplats bekommen?
The bed creaks terribly	Das Bett knarrt furchtbar
	dass bet knarrt foorkhtbar
The bed sags _____	Das Bett biegt sich durch
	dass bet beekt zikh doorkh
Could we have a _____ board to put underneath?	Haben Sie ein Brett zum Drunterlegen?
	harben zee ain bret tsoom droonter laygen?
It's too noisy _____	Es ist zu laut
	ez ist tsoo lowt
We have trouble _____ with bugs/ insects	Wir haben Ärger mit Ungeziefer/Insekten
	veer harben airger mit oongetseefer/ inzekten
This place is full_____ of mosquitoes	Es wimmelt hier von Mücken
	ez vimmelt heer fon mueken
– cockroaches_____	Es wimmelt hier von Kakerlaken
	ez vimmelt heer fon karker larken
– Brits _____	Es wimmelt hier von Briten
	ez vimmelt heer fon britten

.5 Departure

See also 8.2 Settling the bill

I'm leaving tomorrow. _____ Could I settle my bill, please?	Ich reise morgen ab. Könnte ich jetzt bitte abrechnen?
	ikh raizer morgen ap. koennter ikh yetst bitter aprekhnen?
What time should we _____ vacate?	Wann müssen wir den/das/die... verlassen?
	vann muessen veer dayn/dass/dee... fairlassen?
Could I have my deposit/ _____ passport back, please?	Würden Sie mir bitte die Kaution/den Pass wiedergeben?
	vuerden zee meer bitter dee kowtseeoan/dayn pass veeder gayben?
We're in a terrible hurry _____	Wir haben grosse Eile
	veer harben groasser ailer
Could you forward _____ my mail to this address?	Würden Sie mir bitte die Post an diese Adresse nachschicken?
	vuerden zee meer bitter dee posst an deezer adresser nakh shikken?
Could we leave our _____ luggage here until we leave?	Dürfen wir unsere Koffer bis zur Abreise hier stehenlassen?
	duerfen veer oonzere koffer biss tsoor apraizer heer shtayen lassen?
Thanks for your _____ hospitality	Vielen Dank für die Gastlichkeit/die Gastfreundschaft
	feelen dunk fuer dee gastlikh kait/dee gast froynt shaft

Overnight accommodation

Money matters

8 **M**oney matters

● **In general**, banks are open to the public between 9 am and 4.30 pm. Some types of bank, smaller outlets and banks in smaller towns and villages often close for lunch between 12 noon and 2 pm. Banks are closed on a Saturday. To exchange currency a proof of identity is usually required. The sign Geld/wechsel/ausländische Währung indicates that money can be changed. Hotels may also offer exchange facilities but at less favourable rates.

.1 **B**anks

Where can I find a bank/an exchange office around here?	Wo ist hier eine Bank/eine Wechselstube? _vo ist heer ainer bank/ainer vekhsel shtoober?_
Where can I cash this traveller's cheque/giro cheque?	Wo kann ich diesen Reisescheck/Postbarscheck einlösen? _vo kann ikh deezen raizer shekk/postbar shekk ainloezen?_
Can I cash this...here?	Kann ich hier diesen ... einlösen? _kann ikh heer deezen ... ainloezen?_
Can I withdraw money on my credit card here?	Kann ich hier mit einer Kreditkarte Geld bekommen? _kann ikh heer mit ainer kredit karter gelt bekommen?_
What's the minimum/maximum amount?	Was ist das Minimum/Maximum? _vass ist dass minimoom/maksimoom?_
Can I take out less than that?	Darf ich auch weniger abheben? _darf ikh owkh vayniger aphayben?_
I've had some money transferred here. Has it arrived yet?	Ich habe Geld überweisen lassen. Ist es schon eingegangen? _ikh harber gelt ueber vaizen lassen. ist ez shoan ain gegangen?_
These are the details of my bank in the UK	Dies sind die Angaben von meiner Bank in England _deez zint dee angarben fon mainer bank in englant_
This is my bank/giro number	Dies ist meine Kontonummer/Gironummer _deez ist mainer konto noomer/geero noomer_
I'd like to change some money	Ich möchte Geld wechseln _ikh moekhter gelt vekhseln_
– pounds into...	– (englische) Pfund in... _– (englisher) pfoont in..._
– dollars into...	– Dollars in... _– (dollars) in..._
What's the exchange rate?	Wie hoch ist der Wechselkurs? _vee hokh ist dayr vekhsel koors?_
Could you give me some small change with it?	Können Sie mir auch etwas Kleingeld geben? _koennen zee meer owkh etvass klaingelt gayben?_
This is not right	Das stimmt nicht _dass shtimmt nikht_

.2 Settling the bill

Could you put it on _____ Könnten Sie das auf die Rechnung
my bill?   setzen?
                            *koennten zee dass owf dee rekhnoong
                            setsen?*

Does this amount _____ Ist die Bedienung in diesem Betrag
include service?   enthalten?
                         *ist dee bedeenoong in deezem betrark
                         enthalten?*

Can I pay by...? _____ Kann ich mit...bezahlen?
                         kann ikh mit...betsarlen?

Can I pay by credit card?___ Kann ich mit (einer) Kreditkarte bezahlen?
                             kann ikh mit (ainer) kredit karter betsarlen?

Can I pay by traveller's _____ Kann ich mit einem Reisescheck
cheque?   bezahlen?
                                 kann ikh mit ainem raizer shekk betsarlen?

Can I pay with foreign _____ Kann ich in ausländischer Währung
currency?   bezahlen?
                               *kann ikh in owslendisher vayroong
                               betsarlen?*

You've given me too _____ Sie haben mir zuviel/zuwenig
much/you haven't given   (wieder)gegeben
me enough change   *zee harben meer tsoofeel/tsoovaynikh
                            (veeder) gegayben*

Could you check this _____ Würden Sie das noch mal nachrechnen?
again, please?   *vuerden zee dass nokh marl nakh rekhnen?*

Could I have a receipt, _____ Ich hätte gern eine Quittung/den
please?   Kassenzettel
                                *ikh hetter gayrn ainer kvittoong/dayn kassen
                                tsettel*

I don't have enough _____ Ich habe nicht genug Geld bei mir
money on me   *ikh harber nikht genook gelt bai meer*

This is for you _____ Bitte, das ist für Sie
                        bitter, dass ist fuer zee

Keep the change _____ Behalten Sie das Wechselgeld
                        beharlten zee dass vekhselgelt

Post and telephone

9 Post and telephone

9.1 Post

For giros, see 8 Money matters

● **Post offices** are open from Monday to Friday between 8.30 am and 5 pm. In smaller towns the post office closes at lunch. On Saturdays they are open until 12 noon. Stamps are only available at post offices and some hotel receptions. Post boxes are yellow.

Briefmarken stamps Päckchen/Pakete parcels	Postanweisung money orders	Telegramme telegrams

Where's...? — Wo ist...?
vo ist...?

Where's the post office? — Wo ist hier ein Postamt?
vo ist heer ain postamt?

Where's the main post office? — Wo ist die Hauptpost?
vo ist dee howptpost?

Where's the postbox? — Wo ist hier ein Briefkasten?
vo ist heer ain breefkasten?

Which counter should I go to...? — An welchem Schalter kann ich... ?
an velkhem shalter kann ikh...?

– to send a fax — An welchem Schalter kann ich telefaxen?
an velkhem shalter kann ikh telefaksen?

– to change money — An welchem Schalter kann ich Geld wechseln?
an velkhem shalter kann ikh gelt vekhseln?

– to change giro cheques — An welchem Schalter kann ich Schecks einlösen?
an velkhem shalter kann ikh shekks ain loezen?

– for a Telegraph Money Order? — An welchem Schalter kann ich telegrafisch Geld überweisen?
an velkhem shalter kann ikh telegrarfish gelt ueber vaizen?

Poste restante — Postlagernd
postlargernt

Is there any mail for me. My name's... — Ist Post für mich da? Mein Name ist...
ist post fuer mikh dar? main narmer ist...

Stamps

What's the postage for a...to...? — Wieviel muss auf einen/ein(e)...nach...?
veefeel mooss owf ainen/ain(er)...nakh...?

Are there enough stamps on it? — Sind genug Briefmarken drauf?
zint genook breefmarken drowf?

I'd like... ...mark stamps — Ich möchte...Briefmarken zu...
ikh moekhter...breefmarken tsoo...

I'd like to send this... — Ich möchte dies...schicken
ikh moekhter dees...shikken

79

– express _____	Ich möchte dies per Eilboten schicken
	ikh moekhter dees payr ailboaten shikken
– by air mail _____	Ich möchte dies per Luftpost schicken
	ikh moekhter dees payr looftpost shikken
– by registered mail _____	Ich möchte dies per Einschreiben schicken
	ikh moekhter dees payr ainshraiben shikken

Telegram/fax

I'd like to send a _____ telegram to...	Ich möchte ein Telegramm nach... aufgeben
	ikh moekhter ain telegram nakh... owfgayben
How much is that _____ per word?	Wieviel kostet das pro Wort?
	veefeel kostet dass pro vort?
This is the text I want_____ to send	Dies ist der Text des Telegramms
	dees ist dayr tekst dess telegrams
Shall I fill out the form_____ myself?	Soll ich das Formular selbst ausfüllen?
	zoll ikh dass formoolar zelpst owsfuellen?
Can I make photocopies/___ send a fax here?	Kann ich hier fotokopieren/telefaxen?
	kann ikh heer foto kopeeren/telefaksen?
How much is it_____ per page?	Wieviel kostet das pro Seite?
	veefeel kostet dass pro zaiter?

.2 Telephone

See also 1.8 Telephone alphabet

● **All phone booths** offer a direct international service to the UK. To phone the UK dial 0044, plus the UK area code without the first 0. They are either coin phones (10 Pfennig, 50 Pfennig, 1 DM, 5 DM) or card phones. The cards can be bought at post offices. Some telephone booths will also accept credit cards. Phone booths do not accept incoming calls. A reverse-charge call (*ein R-Gespräch*) has to go via the operator. When phoning someone in Germany, you may be greeted with the subscriber's name or with *Hallo* or *Ja*.

Is there a phone box _____ around here?	Ist hier eine Telefonzelle in der Nähe?
	ist heer ainer telefoan tseller in dayr nayher?
Could I use your _____ phone, please?	Dürfte ich Ihr Telefon benutzen?
	duerfter ikh eer telefoan benuetsen?
Do you have a _____ (city/region)...phone directory?	Haben Sie ein Telefonbuch (von der Stadt.../ dem Bezirk...)?
	harben zee ain telefoan bookh (fon dayr shtat.../daym betseerk...)?
Where can I get a _____ phone card?	Wo kann ich eine Telefonkarte kaufen?
	vo kann ikh ainer telefoan karter kowfen?
Could you give me...? _____	Könnten Sie mir...geben?
	koennten zee meer...gayben?
– the number for _____ international directory enquiries	Könnten Sie mir die Nummer der Auslandsauskunft geben?
	koennten zee meer dee noomer dayr owslantsowskoonft gayben?
– the number of room... ___	Könnten Sie mir die Nummer von Zimmer ... geben?
	koennten zee meer dee noomer fon tsimmer ...gayben?

– the international access code	Könnten Sie mir die internationale Nummer geben?
	koennten zee meer dee inter natseeo narle noommer gayben?
– the country code for...	Könnten Sie mir die Ländervorwahl von ... geben?
	koennten zee meer dee lender forvarl fon ... gayben?
– the trunk code for...	Könnten Sie mir die Vorwahl von ... geben?
	koennten zee meer dee forvarl fon ... gayben?
– the number of...	Könnten Sie mir die Rufnummer von ... geben?
	koennten zee meer dee roofnoomer fon ... gayben?
Could you check if this number's correct?	Könnten Sie kontrollieren, ob diese Nummer richtig ist?
	koennten zee kontroleeren, op deezer noomer rikhtikh ist?
Can I dial international direct?	Kann ich automatisch ins Ausland telefonieren?
	kan ikh owtomatish ins owslant telefoaneeren?
Do I have to go through the switchboard?	Muss ich über die Telefonistin telefonieren?
	mooss ikh ueber dee telefoanisstin telefoaneeren?
Do I have to dial '0' first?	Muss ich erst eine Null wählen?
	mooss ikh erst ainer nool vaylen?
Do I have to book my calls?	Muss ich ein Gespräch anmelden?
	mooss ikh ain geshprek anmelden?
Could you dial this number for me, please?	Würden Sie bitte folgende Nummer für mich anrufen?
	vuerden zee bitter folgender noommer fuer mikh anroofen?
Could you put me through to.../extension..., please?	Verbinden Sie mich bitte mit.../Apparat...
	fairbinden zee mikh bitter mit.../apparart...
I'd like to place a reverse-charge call to...	Ich möchte ein R-Gespräch mit...
	ikh moekhter ain air-geshprekh mit...
What's the charge per minute?	Wieviel kostet das pro Minute?
	veefeel kostet dass pro meenooter?
Have there been any calls for me?	Hat jemand für mich angerufen?
	hat yaymant fuer mikh angeroofen?

The conversation

Hello, this is...	Guten Tag, ... hier
	gooten tark, ... heer
Who is this, please?	Mit wem spreche ich?
	mit vaym shprekher ikh?
Is this...?	Spreche ich mit...?
	shprekher ikh mit...?
I'm sorry, I've dialled the wrong number	Entschuldigung, ich habe mich verwählt
	ent shool digung, ikh harber mikh fairvaylt

I can't hear you _____	Ich kann Sie nicht verstehen *ikh kann zee nikht fairshtayhen*
I'd like to speak to... _____	Ich möchte ... sprechen *ikh moekhter ... shprekhen*
Extension..., please_____	Apparat ... bitte *apparart ... bitter*
Could you ask him/her_____ to call me back?	Er/sie möchte mich bitte zurückrufen *ayr/zee moekhter mikh bitter tsooruekh roofen*
My name's... _____ My number's...	Mein Name ist... Meine Nummer ist... *main narmer ist... mainer noommer ist...*
I'll call back tomorrow _____	Ich rufe ihn/sie morgen wieder an *ikh roofer een/zee morgen veeder an*

German	English
Telefon für Sie _____	There's a phone call for you
Sie müssen erst eine Null wählen _____	You have to dial '0' first
(Einen) Augenblick bitte _____	One moment, please
Es antwortet niemand_____	There's no answer
Die Nummer ist besetzt _____	The line's engaged
Wollen Sie warten? _____	Do you want to hold?
Ich verbinde _____	Putting you through
Sie haben die falsche Nummer _____ (gewählt)	You've got a wrong number
Er/sie ist im Augenblick nicht da/im _____ Haus	He's/she's not here right now
Er/sie ist...wieder zu erreichen _____	He'll/she'll be back...
Dies ist der Anrufbeantworter von..._____	This is the answering machine of...

Shopping

10 Shopping

● **Opening times:** Supermarkets and department stores are open Monday to Friday 8.30/9 am - 5.30/6pm, on Saturdays they are usually closed after 2 pm. However, every first Saturday of the month is a *langer Samstag* (long Saturday) which means that shops stay open until about 6pm. In many larger towns shops stay open until 8.30 pm on a Thursday. Smaller shops may close for lunch between 12 noon and 2 pm and on Wednesday afternoons.

Andenkenladen	Heimwerker Markt	Schuhgeschäft
souvenir shop	DIY-store	shoe shop
Antiquitäten	Kaufhaus	Schuhmacher/
antiques	department store	Schuster
Bäckerei	Konditorei	cobbler
bakery	cake shop	Second-Hand-Laden
Beleuchtung	Kosmetiksalon	second hand goods
lighting	beauty parlour	Spielzeuggeschäft
Buchhandlung	Kürschner	toy shop
bookshop	furrier	Spirituosenhandlung
Drogerie	Kurzwarenhandlung	off licence
chemist	haberdashery	Sportartikel
Einkaufszentrum	Laden	sports shop
shopping centre	shop	Süsswaren
Eisenwarengeschäft	Metzgerei	sweet shop
hardware store	butcher's	Tante-Emma-Laden
Elektrogeräte	Molkereigeschäft	corner shop
electrical appliances	dairy	Trafik
Fahrradgeschäft	Münzwäscherei	tobacconist
cycle shop	laundrette	Uhrengeschäft
Feinkost	Musikalienhandlung	clock shop/jeweller
delicatessen	music shop	Wäscherei
Fischgeschäft	Obst und Gemüse	laundry
fishmonger	greengrocer	Zoohandlung
Flohmarkt	Ökoladen	pet shop
fleamarket	health food shop	
Florist	Optiker	
florist	opticians	
Frisör	Pelze	
hairdresser	fur	
Gärtnerei	Rauchwarengeschäft	
nursery	tobacconist	
Geschäft	Raumausstat-	
shop	tung(shaus)	
Getränkemarkt	interior decorator	
drinks store	Reinigung	
Handarbeitsgeschäft	dry cleaner	
needle work and	Schallplatten-	
wool shop	geschäft	
Handlung	record shop	
dealer	Schlachter	
Haushaltswaren	butcher	
household goods	Schmuck	
	jeweller	

🔟 .1 **S**hopping conversations

Where can I get...? _____	In welchem Geschäft kann ich ... bekommen?
	in velkhem gesheft kan ikh ... bekommen?
When does this shop _____ open?	Wann hat dieses Geschäft geöffnet?
	van hat deezez gesheft geoeffnet?
Could you tell me _____ where the...department is?	Können Sie mir sagen, wo die ... Abteilung ist?
	koennen zee meer zargen vo dee ... aptailoong ist?
Could you help me, _____ please? I'm looking for...	Können Sie mir bitte helfen? Ich suche...
	koennen zee meer bitter helfen? ikh zookher...
Do you sell English/ _____ American newspapers?	Verkaufen Sie englische/amerikanische Zeitungen?
	fairkowfen zee englisher/amerikarnisher tsai toongen?

Werden Sie schon bedient? _____	**Are you being served?**

No, I'd like... _____	Nein, ich möchte...
	nain, ikh moekhter...
I'm just looking, _____ if that's all right	Ich möchte mich nur mal umsehen
	ikh moekhter mikh noor marl oom zayhen

Sonst noch (et)was? _____	**Anything else?**

Yes, I'd also like... _____	Ja, bitte auch noch...
	yar, bitter owkh nokh...
No, thank you. That's all ___	Nein, danke. Das ist alles
	nain, dunker. dass ist alles
Could you show me...? ___	Können Sie mir ... zeigen?
	koennen zee meer ... tsaigen?
I'd prefer... _____	Ich möchte lieber...
	ikh moekhter leeber...
This is not what I'm _____ looking for	Das ist nicht, was ich suche
	dass ist nikht vass ikh zookher
I'll keep looking _____	Ich sehe mich erst noch mal weiter um
	ikh zayher mikh airst nokh marl vaiter oom
Do you have _____ something...?	Haben Sie nicht etwas, vass...ist?
	harben zee nikht etvass, vass...ist?
– less expensive? _____	Haben Sie nicht etwas Billigeres?
	harben zee nikht etvass billigerez?
– something smaller? _____	Haben Sie nicht etwas Kleineres?
	harben zee nikht etvass klainerez?
– something larger? _____	Haben Sie nicht etwas Grösseres?
	harben zee nikht etvass groerserez?
I'll take this one _____	Ich nehme dies
	ikh naymer deez
Does it come with _____ instructions?	Ist eine Gebrauchsanweisung dabei?
	ist ainer gebrowkhs anvai zoong darbai?

Shopping

It's too expensive _____	Ich finde es zu teuer
	ikh finder ez tsoo toyer
I'll give you... _____	Ich biete Ihnen...
	ikh beeter eenen...
Could you keep this for ____ me? I'll come back for it later	Kann ich ihn/sie/es hierlassen? Ich hole ihn/sie/es nachher ab
	kan ikh een/zee/es heerlassen? ikh hoaler een/zee/es nakhherr ap
Have you got a bag _____ for me, please?	Haben Sie bitte eine Tüte für mich?
	harben zee bitter ainer tueter fuer mikh?
Could you giftwrap _____ it, please?	Könnten Sie es bitte in Geschenkpapier einpacken?
	koennten zee ez bitter in geshenk papeer ainpakken?

(Es) tut mir leid, das haben/ _____ führen wir nicht	I'm sorry, we don't have that
(Es) tut mir leid, das ist ausverkauft ____	I'm sorry, we're sold out
Tut mir leid, das kriegen wir erst... _____ wieder rein	I'm sorry, that won't be in until...
Sie können an der Kasse zahlen _____	You can pay at the cash desk
Wir nehmen keine Kreditkarten an _____	We don't accept credit cards
Wir nehmen keine Reiseschecks an ____	We don't accept traveller's cheques
Wir nehmen kein ausländisches _____ Geld/keine Fremdwährungen an	We don't accept foreign currency

10 .2 Food

I'd like a hundred _____ grams of..., please	Hundert Gramm...bitte
	hoondert gramm...bitter
– five hundred grams/ ____ half a kilo of...	Fünfhundert Gramm/ein halbes Kilo/(ein Pfund) ... bitte
	fuenfhoondert gramm/ain halbes keelo/(ain pfoont)...bitter
– a kilo of... _____	Ein Kilo ... bitte
	ain keelo...bitter
Could you...it for me, _____ please?	Würden Sie es mir bitte...?
	vuerden zee es meer bitter...?
Could you slice it/ _____ dice it for me, please?	Würden Sie es mir bitte in Scheiben/Stücke/(kleine)Würfel schneiden?
	vuerden zee es meer bitter in shaiben/shtueker/(klainer) vuerfel shnaiden?
Could you grate it _____ for me, please?	Würden Sie es mir bitte reiben?
	vuerden zee es meer bitter raiben?
Can I order it? _____	Kann ich es bestellen?
	kan ikh es beshtellen?
I'll pick it up tomorrow/ ____ at...	Ich hole es morgen/um...Uhr ab
	ikh hoaler es morgen/oom...oor ap
Can you eat/drink this? ____	Kann man das essen/trinken?
	kan man dass essen/trinken?

10 .3 Clothing and shoes

I saw something in the ___ window. Shall I point it out?	Ich habe im Schaufenster etwas gesehen. Soll ich es Ihnen zeigen? *ikh harber im showfenster etvass gesayhen. zoll ikh ez eenen tsaigen?*
I'd like something to_____ go with this	Ich möchte gern etwas, was hierzu passt *ikh moekhter gayrn etvass, vass heertsoo passt*
Do you have shoes _____ to match this colour?	Haben Sie Schuhe in derselben Farbe wie diese hier? *harben zee shooer in derselben farber vee deezer heer?*
I'm a size...in the UK_____	In England habe ich Grösse... *in englant harber ikh groesser...*
Can I try this on? _____	Darf ich dies anprobieren? *darf ikh dees anprobeeren?*
Where's the fitting room? __	Wo ist die Anprobe? *vo ist dee anprober?*
It doesn't fit_____	Es passt mir nicht *es passt meer nikht*
This is the right size _____	Das ist die richtige Grösse *dass ist dee rikhtiger groesser*
It doesn't suit me_____	Es steht mir nicht *es shtayt meer nikht*
Do you have this/ _____ these in...?	Haben Sie dies/diese auch in...? *harben zee dees/deezer owkh in...?*
The heel's too high/low ____	Ich finde den Absatz zu hoch/niedrig *ikh finder den apzats tsoo hokh/needrikh*
Is this/are these _____ genuine leather?	Ist dies/sind diese aus echtem Leder? *ist dees/zint deezer ows ekhtem layder?*
I'm looking for a..._____ for a...-year-old baby/child	Ich suche ein(en)/eine ... für ein Baby/Kind von ... Jahren *ikh zookher ain(en)/ainer ... fuer ain baby/kint fon ... yahren*
I'd like a... _____	Ich hätte gern ein(en)/eine ... aus *ikh hetter gayrn ain(en)/ainer ... ows*
– silk _____	Ich hätte gern ein(en)/eine ... aus Seide *ikh hetter gayrn ain(en)/ainer ... ows zaider*
– cotton _____	Ich hätte gern ein(en)/eine ... aus Baumwolle *ikh hetter gayrn ain(en)/ainer ... ows bowmvoller*
– woollen _____	Ich hätte gern ein(en)/eine ... aus Wolle *ikh hetter gayrn ain(en)/ainer ... ows voller*
– linen_____	Ich hätte gern ein(en)/eine ... aus Leinen *ikh hetter gayrn ain(en)/ainer ... ows lainen*
What temperature_____ can I wash it at?	Bei welcher Temperatur kann ich es waschen? *bai velkher temperatoor kan ikh es vashen?*
Will it shrink in the _____ wash?	Läuft es (in der Wäsche) ein? *loyft es (in der wesher) ain?*

Shopping

Chemisch reinigen	Maschinenwaschbar	Nicht bügeln
Dry clean	Machine washable	Do not iron
Handwäsche	Nass aufhängen	Nicht schleudern
Hand wash	Drip dry	Do not spin

At the cobbler

Could you mend _____ these shoes?	Können Sie diese Schuhe reparieren? *koennen zee deezer shooer repareeren?*
Could you put new _____ soles/heels on these?	Können Sie diese hier versohlen/die Absätze erneuern? *koennen zee deezer heer fairzoalen/dee apsetzer ernoyern?*
When will they be _____ ready?	Wann sind sie fertig? *vann zint zee fairtikh?*
I'd like..., please _____	Ich möchte (gern)... *ikh moekhter (gayrn)...*
– a tin of shoe polish _____	Ich möchte gern eine Dose Schuhcreme *ikh moekhter gayrn ainer doazer shookremer*
– a pair of shoelaces_____	Ich möchte gern ein Paar Schuhbänder *ikh moekhter gayrn ain par shoobender*

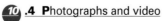 .4 Photographs and video

I'd like a film for this_____ camera, please	Ich möchte einen Film für diesen Apparat *ikh moekhter ainen film fuer deezen apparart*
– a cartridge _____	Ich möchte eine Cassette *ikh moekhter ainer kassetter*
– a one twenty-six_____ cartridge	Ich möchte eine 126er Cassette *ikh moekhter ainer ain hoondert zekhs oont tvantsiger kassetter*
– a slide film _____	Ich möchte einen Diafilm *ikh moekhter ainen diafilm*
– a film cartridge _____	Ich möchte eine Filmcassette *ikh moekhter ainer filmkassetter*
– a videotape _____	Ich möchte ein Videoband *ikh moekhter ain veedeeo bant*
colour/black and white_____	Farbe/schwarzweiss *farber/shvarts vaiss*
super eight _____	Super 8 *zooper akht*
12/24/36 exposures _____	12/24/36 Aufnahmen *tsvoelf/feer oont tsvantsikh/zekhs oont draissikh owfnarmen*
ASA/DIN number_____	ISO Wert *eessoh vayrt*
daylight film _____	(der) Tageslichtfilm *(dayr) targes likht film*
film for artificial light _____	(der) Kunstlichtfilm *(dayr) koonst likht film*

Problems

Could you load the _____ film for me, please?	Würden Sie den Film bitte für mich einlegen? *vuerden zee den film bitter fuer mikh ainlaygen?*
Could you take the film _____ out for me, please?	Würden Sie bitte den Film für mich aus der Kamera nehmen? *vuerden zee bitter dayn film fuer mikh ows der kamerar naymen?*
Should I replace _____ the batteries?	Muss ich die Batterien auswechseln? *mooss ikh dee battereeyen ows vekhseln?*
Could you have a look _____ at my camera, please? It's not working	Könnten Sie sich bitte mal die Kamera ansehen? Sie funktioniert nicht mehr *koennten zee zikh bitter marl dee kamerar anzayhen? zee foonk tseeoneert nikht mair*
The...is broken _____	Der/die/das ... ist kaputt *dayr/dee/dass ... ist kapoott*
The film's jammed _____	Der Film klemmt *dayr film klemmt*
The film's broken _____	Der Film ist gerissen *dayr film ist gerissen*
The flash isn't working _____	Das Blitzlicht funktioniert nicht *dass blits likht foonk tseeoneert nikht*
I'd like to have this film _____ developed/printed, please	Ich möchte diesen Film entwickeln/abziehen lassen *ikh moekhter deezen film entvikkeln/ap tseeyen lassen*
I'd like...prints from _____ each negative	Ich möchte von jedem Negativ ... Abzüge *ikh moekhter fon yaydem negateef ... aptsueger*
glossy/mat _____	glänzend/matt *glentsent/mat*
7x5 _____	Sieben mal fünf *zeeben marl fuenf*
I'd like to reorder _____ these photos	Ich möchte diese Fotos nachbestellen *ikh moekhter deezer fotos nakh beshtellen*
I'd like to have this _____ photo enlarged	Ich möchte dieses Foto vergrössern lassen *ikh moekhter deezez foto fair groessern lassen*
How much is _____ processing?	Wieviel kostet das Entwickeln? *veefeel kostet dass entvikkeln?*
– printing _____	Wieviel kosten die Abzüge? *veefeel kosten dee aptsueger?*
– it to reorder _____	Wieviel kostet die Nachbestellung? *veefeel kostet dee nakh beshtelloong?*
– the enlargement _____	Wieviel kostet die Vergrösserung? *veefeel kostet dee fair groesseroong?*
When will they _____ be ready?	Wann sind sie fertig? *vann zint zee fairtikh?*

Shopping

89

Do I have to make an _____ appointment?	Muss ich einen Termin machen? *mooss ikh ainen termeen makhen?*
Can I come in straight _____ away?	Kann ich sofort drankommen? *kann ikh zofort drannkommen?*
How long will I have_____ to wait?	Wie lange muss ich warten? *vee langer mooss ikh varten?*
I'd like a shampoo/ _____ haircut	Ich möchte mir die Haare waschen/schneiden lassen *ikh moekhter meer dee haarer vashen/shnaiden lassen*
I'd like a shampoo for _____ oily/dry hair, please	Ein Shampoo gegen fettes/trockenes Haar bitte *ain shampoo gaygen fettez/trokkenez haar bitter*
an anti-dandruff_____ shampoo	Ein Shampoo gegen Schuppen bitte *ain shampoo gaygen shooppen bitter*
– a shampoo for_____ permed/coloured hair	Ein Shampoo für dauergewelltes/gefärbtes Haar bitte *ain shampoo fuer dower gevelltes/gefayrptes har bitter*
– a colour rinse shampoo _	Ein Farbshampoo bitte *ain farp shampoo bitter*
– a shampoo with _____ conditioner	Ein Shampoo mit einem Pflegemittel bitte *ain shampoo mit ainem pflayger mittel bitter*
– highlights _____	Blonde Strähnchen bitte *blonder shtraynkhen bitter*
Do you have a colour_____ chart, please?	Hätten Sie eine Farbenkarte? *hetten zee ainer farben karter?*
I want to keep it the _____ same colour	Ich möchte die Farbe behalten *ikh moekhter dee farber behalten*
I'd like it darker/lighter_____	Ich möchte es dunkler/heller haben *ikh moekhter ez dunkler/heller harben*
I'd like/I don't want _____ hairspray	Ich möchte (keinen) Haarfestiger *ikh moekhter (kainen) haarfestigger*
– gel_____	Ich möchte (kein) Gel *ikh moekhter (kain) jell*
– lotion _____	Ich möchte (keine) Lotion *ikh moekhter (kainer) loatseeyoan*
I'd like a short fringe _____	Ich möchte meinen Pony kurz tragen *ikh moekhter mainen pony koorts tragen*
Not too short at the back _	Hinten nicht zu kurz schneiden bitte *hinten nikht tsoo koorts shnaiden bitter*
Not too long here _____	Hier bitte nicht zu lang *heer bitter nikht tsoo lang*
I'd like/I don't want _____ (many) curls	Ich möchte (nicht zuviel) Locken *ikh moekhter (nikht tsoofeel) locken*
It needs a little/_____ a lot taken off	Bitte schneiden Sie ein kleines bisschen/ein gutes Stück ab *bitter shnaiden zee ain klainez bisskhen/ain gootez shtook ap*
I'd like it the same_____ as in this photo	Ich möchte eine Frisur wie auf diesem Foto *ikh moekhter ainer frizoor vee owf deezem foto*

Could you put the _____ drier up/down a bit?	Könnten Sie die Haube etwas höher/niedriger einstellen?
	koennten zee dee howber etvass hoeher/needriger ain shtellen?
I'd like a facial_____	Ich möchte eine Gesichtsmaske
	ikh moekhter ainer gezikhts masker
– a manicure _____	Ich möchte mich maniküren lassen
	ikh moekhter mikh manni kueren lassen
– a massage _____	Ich möchte eine Massage

Welchen Schnitt möchten Sie? _____	How do you want it cut?
Welches Modell möchten Sie? _____	What style did you have in mind?
Welche Farbe soll es sein?_____	What colour did you want it?
Ist das die richtige Temperatur? _____	Is the temperature all right for you?
Wünschen Sie etwas zu(m) Lesen? _____	Would you like something to read?
Wünschen Sie etwas zu trinken? _____	Would you like a drink?
Ist es so richtig? _____	Is this what you had in mind?

	ikh moekhter ainer massarjer
Could you trim_____ my fringe?	Würden Sie mir bitte den Pony kürzen?
	vuerden zee meer bitter dayn pony kuertsen?
my beard/	Würden Sie mir bitte den
my moustache? _____	Bart/Schnurrbart stutzen?
	vuerden zee meer bitter dayn bart/shnoorbart shtootsen?
I'd like a shave, please_____	Rasieren bitte
	razeeren bitter
I'd like a wet shave, _____ please	Ich möchte bitte nass rasiert werden
	ikh moekhter bitter nass razeert verden

At the Tourist Information Centre

At the Tourist Information Centre

11 .1 Places of interest

Where's the Tourist Information, please?	Wo ist der Fremdenverkehrsverein? *vo ist dayr fremden fayr kayrs fairrain?*
Do you have a city map?	Haben Sie einen Stadtplan? *harben zee ainen shtatplarn?*
Could you give me some information about...?	Können Sie mir Auskunft geben über...? *koennen zee meer owskoonft gayben ueber...?*
How much is that?	Wieviel kostet das? *veefeel kostet dass?*
What are the main places of interest?	Welches sind die wichtigsten Sehenswürdigkeiten? *velkhez zint dee vikhtikhsten zayhens vuerdikh kaiten?*
Could you point them out on the map?	Könnten Sie mir die auf dem Plan zeigen? *koennten zee meer dee owf daym plarn tsaigen?*
What do you recommend?	Was empfehlen Sie uns? *vass empfaylen zee oons?*
We'll be here for a few hours	Wir bleiben hier ein paar Stunden *veer blaiben heer ain par shtoonden*
– a day	Wir bleiben hier einen Tag *veer blaiben heer ainen tark*
– a week	Wir bleiben hier eine Woche *veer blaiben heer ainer vokher*
We're interested in...	Wir interessieren uns für... *veer interesseeren oons fuer...*
Is there a scenic walk around the city?	Können wir einen Stadtrundgang machen? *koennen veer ainen shtat roont gang makhen?*
How long does it take?	Wie lange dauert der? *vee langer dowert dayr?*
Where does it start/end?	Wo ist der Anfang/das Ende? *vo ist der anfang/dass ender?*
Are there any boat cruises here?	Gibt es hier Rundfahrtboote/-schiffe/Ausflugsschiffe? *gipt es heer roont fahrt boater/shiffer/-ows flooks shiffer?*
Where can we board?	Wo können wir an Bord gehen? *vo koennen veer an bort gayhen?*
Are there any bus tours?	Gibt es Busrundfahrten? *gipt es boos roont fahrten?*
Where do we get on?	Wo müssen wir einsteigen? *vo muessen veer ainshtaigen?*
Is there a guide who speaks English?	Gibt es einen englisch sprechenden Führer? *gipt ez ainen english shprekhenden fuerer?*
Are there any excursions?	Gibt es Ausflüge? *gipt ez owsflueger?*

English	German
What trips can we take around the area?	Welche Ausflüge in die Umgebung kann man machen? *velkher owsflooger in dee oom gay boong kann man makhen?*
Where do they go to?	Wohin gehen die? *vohin gayhen dee?*
We'd like to go to...	Wir möchten nach... *veer moekhten nakh...*
How long is the trip?	Wie lange dauert der Ausflug? *vee langer dowert dayr owsflook?*
How long do we stay in...?	Wie lange bleiben wir in...? *vee langer blaiben veer in...?*
Are there any guided tours?	Gibt es Führungen? *gipt ez fyueroongen?*
How much free time will we have there?	Wieviel Freizeit haben wir da? *veefeel fraitsait harben veer dar?*
We want to go hiking	Wir möchten eine Wanderung machen *veer moekhten ainer vanderoong makhen*
Can we hire a guide?	Können wir einen Führer engagieren? *koennen veer ainen fuerer engajeeren?*
Can I book mountain huts?	Kann ich einen Platz in einer (Berg)hütte reservieren lassen? *kann ikh ainen plats in ainer (berg)hueter rezerveeren lassen?*
What time does... open/close?	Wann öffnet/schliesst (der/die/das)...? *van oeffnet/shleest (dayr/dee/dass)...?*
What days is...open/ closed?	An welchen Tagen ist der/die/das... geöffnet/geschlossen? *an velkhen targen ist dayr/dee/dass ... geoeffnet/geshlossen?*
What's the admission price?	Wieviel kostet der Eintritt? *veefeel kostet dayr aintrit?*
Is there a group discount?	Gibt es Gruppenermässigung? *gipt es groopen ermayssigoong?*
Is there a child discount?	Gibt es Ermässigung für Kinder? *gipt es ermayssigoong fuer kinder?*
Is there a discount for pensioners?	Gibt es Ermässigung für Senioren? *gipt es ermayssigoong fuer zeneeoren?*
Can I take (flash) photos/can I film here?	Darf ich hier (mit Blitzlicht) fotografieren/filmen? *darf ikh heer (mit blitslikht) foto grafeeren/filmen?*
Do you have any postcards of...?	Verkaufen Sie Ansichtskarten von dem/ der...? *fayrkowfen zee an sikhts karten fon daym/ dayr...?*
Do you have an English...?	Haben Sie ein(en)/eine ... auf englisch? *harben zee ain(en)/ainer ... owf english?*
– an English catalogue?	Haben Sie einen Katalog auf englisch? *harben zee ainen kataloak owf english?*
– an English programme?	Haben Sie ein Programm auf englisch? *harben zee ain program owf english?*
– an English brochure?	Haben Sie eine Broschüre auf englisch? *harben zee ainer broashoorer owf english?*

.2 Going out

● **At the cinema** most films are dubbed (*synchronisiert*). In larger towns and cities as well as art cinemas subtitled versions are often screened, advertised as *Original mit Untertiteln*.

Do you have this _____ week's/month's entertainment guide?	Haben Sie den Veranstaltungskalender von dieser Woche/diesem Monat? *harben zee den fairan shtal toongs kalen der fon deezer vokher/deezem moanart?*
What's on tonight? _____	Was für Veranstaltungen gibt es heute abend? *vass fuer fairan shtal toongen gipt es hoyter arbent?*
We want to go to... _____	Wir möchten in den/ins/in die... *veer moekhten in dayn/ins/in dee...*
Which films are _____ showing?	Welche Filme werden gespielt? *velkher filmer vairden geshpeelt?*
What sort of film is that?___	Was für ein Film ist das? *vass fuer ain film ist dass?*
rated suitable for _____ the whole family	für jedes Alter *fuer yaydez alter*
rated not suitable for _____ children under 12/16 years	ab 12/16 Jahre(n) *ap tsvoelf/zekh tsayn yahre(n)*
original version _____	Originalfassung *origginaal fassoong*
subtitled _____	untertitelt *oonter teetelt*
dubbed _____	synchronisiert *suen khro nee zeert*
Is it a continuous _____ showing?	Ist es eine durchgehende Vorführung? *ist es ainer doorkh gayhender for fue roong?*
What's on at...? _____	Was gibt es in...? *vass gipt es in...?*
– the theatre? _____	Was gibt es im Theater? *vass gipt es im tayarter?*
– the concert hall?_____	Was gibt es in der Konzerthalle/im Konzertsaal? *vass gipt es in dayr kontsert haller/im kontsert zarl?*
– the opera? _____	Was gibt es in der Oper? *vass gipt es in dayr oaper?*
Where can I find a good ___ disco around here?	Wo gibt es hier eine gute Disko? *vo gipt es heer ainer gooter disko?*
Is it members only? _____	Muss man Mitglied sein? *mooss man mittgleet zain?*
Where can I find a good ___ nightclub around here?	Wo gibt es einen guten Nachtklub? *vo gipt es ainen gooten nakht kloop?*
Is it evening wear only? ___	Ist Abendkleidung Zwang? *ist arbent klai doong tsvang?*
Should I/we dress up? _____	Ist Abendkleidung erwünscht? *ist arbent klai doong errvuensht?*
What time does the _____ show start?	Wann beginnt die Show? *vann begint dee shoa?*

95

When's the next soccer ____ match?	Wann ist das nächste Fussballspiel? *van ist dass nekster foos barl shpeel?*
Who's playing?_____	Wer spielt gegen wen? *vayr shpeelt gaygen vayn?*
I'd like a _____ female/male escort for tonight. Could you arrange that for me?	Ich möchte für heute abend weibliche/männliche Begleitung. Können Sie mir die besorgen? *ikh moekhter fuer hoyter arbent vai plikher/mennlikher beglaitung. koennen zee meer dee bezorgen?*

11.3 Booking tickets

Could you book some ____ tickets for us?	Können Sie für uns reservieren? *koennen zee fuer oons rezerveeren?*
We'd like to book... _____ seats/a table...	Wir möchten...Plätze/einen Tisch...reservieren *veer moekhten...pletzer/ainen tish...rezerveeren*
– in the stalls_____	Wir möchten...Plätze/einen Tisch im Parkett reservieren *veer moekhten...pletzer/ainen tish im parkett rezerveeren*
– on the balcony _____	Wir möchten...Balkonplätze/einen Tisch auf dem Balkon reservieren *veer moekhten...balkoanpletzer/ainen tish owf daym balkoan rezerveeren*
– box seats _____	Wir möchten...Logenplätze reservieren *veer moekhten...loagen pletzer rezerveeren*
– seats at the front _____	Bitte Plätze vorn *bitter pletser forn*
– seats in the middle _____	Bitte Plätze in der Mitte *bitter pletser in der mitter*
– seats at the back_____	Bitte Plätze hinten *bitter pletser hinten*
Could I book...seats for ____ the...o'clock performance?	Kann ich...Plätze für die Vorstellung von...Uhr reservieren lassen? *kan ikh...pletser fuer dee for shtel loong fon ...oohr rezerveeren lassen?*
Are there any seats left ____ for tonight?	Gibt es noch Karten für heute abend? *gipt es nokh karten fuer hoyter arbent?*
How much is a ticket? ____	Wieviel kostet eine Karte? *veefeel kostet ainer karter?*
When can I pick the _____ tickets up?	Wann kann ich die Karten abholen? *van kan ikh dee karten aphoalen?*
I've got a reservation _____	Ich habe reserviert *ikh harber rezerveert*
My name's... _____	Mein Name ist... *main narmer ist...*

Für welche Vorstellung möchten Sie _____ reservieren?	Which performance do you want to book for?
Welche Plätze bitte? _____	Where would you like to sit?
Die Vorstellung ist ausverkauft _____	Everything's sold out
Es gibt nur noch Stehplätze _____	It's standing room only
Es gibt nur noch Balkonplätze _____	We've only got balcony seats left
...gibt es noch eine Sondervorstellung _____	...there is another special performance
Es gibt nur noch Plätze im Parkett _____	We've only got stalls seats left
Es gibt nur noch Plätze in den... _____ vorderen Reihen	We've only got seats left in the...front rows
Es gibt nur noch Plätze in den... _____ hinteren Reihen	We've only got seats left in the...back rows
Wieviel Plätze wünschen Sie? _____	How many seats would you like?
Sie müssen die Karten vor...Uhr _____ abholen	You'll have to pick up the tickets before...o'clock
Ihre Eintrittskarten bitte _____	Tickets, please
Sie sitzen auf den falschen Plätzen _____	You're in the wrong seats

Sports

12 Sports

12.1 Sporting questions

Where can we... around here?	Wo können wir hier...?
	vo koennen veer heer...?
Is there a... around here?	Gibt es hier in der Nähe ein(en)/eine...?
	gipt es heer in dayr nayher ain(en)/ainer...?
Can I hire a...here?	Kann ich hier ein(en)/eine...mieten/leihen?
	kan ikh heer ain(en)/ainer...meeten/laihen?
Can I take...lessons?	Kann ich ...Stunden nehmen?
	kan ikh ... shtoonden naymen?
How much is that per hour/per day/a turn?	Wieviel kostet das pro Stunde/Tag/Mal?
	veefeel kostet dass pro shtoonder/tark/marl?
Do I need a permit for that?	Braucht man dafür einen Schein/eine Genehmigung?
	browkht man darfuer ainen shain/ainer genay mi goong?
Where can I get the permit?	Wo kann ich die Genehmigung bekommen?
	vo kan ikh dee genay mi goong bekommen?

12.2 By the waterfront

Is it a long way to the sea still?	Ist es noch weit bis ans Meer?
	ist es nokh vait biss ans meer?
Is there a...around here?	Gibt es hier in der Nähe ein... ?
	gipt es heer in dayr nayher ain... ?
-an outdoor/indoor/ public swimming pool	Gibt es hier in der Nähe ein (openair pool) Freibad/(indoor pool) Hallenbad/(public pool) eine Badeanstalt?
	gipt es heer in dayr nayher ain fraibart/ainer hallen bart/ainer barder an shalt/?
– a sandy beach	Gibt es hier in der Nähe einen Sandstrand?
	gipt ez heer in dayr nayher ainen sant shtrant?
– a nudist beach	Gibt es hier in der Nähe einen Nacktbadestrand?
	gipt ez heer in dayr nayher ainen nakt barder shtrant?
– mooring	Gibt es hier in der Nähe einen Anlegeplatz?
	gipt ez heer in dayr nayher ainen anlayger plats?
Are there any rocks here?	Sind hier Felsen?
	zint heer felzen?
When's high/low tide?	Wann ist Flut/Ebbe?
	van ist floot/ebber?
What's the water temperature?	Welche Temperatur hat das Wasser?
	velkher temperatoor hat dass vasser?
Is it (very) deep here?	Ist es hier (sehr) tief?
	ist ez heer (zayr) teef?
Can you stand here?	Kann man hier stehen?
	kan man heer shtayen?
Is it safe to swim here?	Kann man/(können Kinder) hier ungefährdet schwimmen?
	kan man/(koennen kinder) heer ungefayrdet shvimmen?
Are there any currents?	Gibt es Strömungen?
	gipt ez shtroe moongen?

Sports

Are there any rapids/ _____ waterfalls in this river?	Hat dieser Fluss Stromschnellen/Wasserfälle?
	hat deezer flooss shtrom shnellen/vasser feller?
What does that flag/ _____ buoy mean?	Was bedeutet die Flagge/Boje dort?
	vass bedoytet dee flagger/boayer dort?
Is there a life guard _____ on duty here?	Gibt es hier einen Bademeister, der aufpasst?
	gipt es heer ainen barder maister, der owfpasst?
Are dogs allowed here? _____	Sind hier Hunde erlaubt?
	zint heer hoonder erlowpt?
Is camping on the _____ beach allowed?	Darf man hier am Strand campen?
	darf man heer am shtrant kampen?
Are we allowed to _____ build a fire here?	Darf man hier Feuer machen?
	darf man heer foyer makhen?

Achtung! Gefahr!	Angeln verboten	Nur mit Genehmigung
Danger	No fishing	Permits only
Angeln erlaubt	Baden verboten	Surfen verboten
Fishing water	No swimming	No surfing

 .3 In the snow

Can I take ski lessons _____ here?	Kann ich hier Skistunden nehmen?
	kan ikh heer shee shtoonden naymen?
for beginners/advanced _____	für Anfänger/(etwas) Fortgeschrittene
	fuer anfenger/(etvass) fortgeshrittenner
How large are the _____ groups?	Wie gross sind die Gruppen?
	vee groass zint dee grooppen?
What language are _____ the classes in?	In welcher Sprache werden die Stunden gegeben?
	in velkher shprakher verden dee shtoonden gegayben?
I'd like a lift pass, _____ please	Ich möchte einen Ski(lift)pass
	ikh moekhter ainen shee(lift)pass
Must I give you a _____ passport photo?	Muss ich ein Passbild abgeben?
	mooss ikh ain passbilt apgayben?
Where can I have a _____ passport photo taken?	Wo kann ich ein Passbild machen lassen?
	vo kan ikh ain passbilt makhen lassen?
Where are the _____ beginners' slopes?	Wo sind die Skipisten für Anfänger? (jokey): Wo ist der Idiotenhügel?)
	vo zint dee shee pisten fuer anfenger?
	vo ist dayr eedeeoea ten huegel?
Are there any runs for cross-country skiing?	Gibt es hier in der Nähe Loipen?
	gipt ez heer in dayr nayher loypen?
Have the cross-country _____ runs been marked?	Sind die Loipen beschildert?
	zint dee loypen beshildert?
Are the...in operation? _____	Sind die...geöffnet?
	zint dee...geoeffnet?
– the ski lifts _____	Sind die Skilifte geöffnet?
	zint dee sheelifter geoeffnet?
– the chair lifts _____	Sind die Sessellifte geöffnet?
	zint dee zessel lifter geoeffnet?
Are the slopes usable? _____	Sind die Pisten offen?
	zint dee pisten offen?
Are the cross-country _____ runs usable?	Sind die Loipen offen?
	zint dee loypen offen?

Sports

Sickness

13 **S**ickness

13.1 **C**all (fetch) the doctor

Could you call/fetch a_____ doctor quickly, please?	Rufen/holen Sie bitte schnell einen Arzt
	roofen/hoalen zee bitter shnell ainen artst
When does the doctor _____ have surgery?	Wann hat der Arzt Sprechstunde?
	van hat dayr artst shprekh shtoonder?
When can the doctor _____ come?	Wann kann der Arzt kommen?
	van kan dayr artst kommen?
I'd like to make an_____ appointment to see the doctor	Können Sie für mich einen Termin beim Arzt machen?
	koennen zee fuer mikh ainen tairmeen baim artst makhen?
I've got an appointment ___ to see the doctor at...	Ich habe um...Uhr einen Termin beim Arzt
	ikh harber oom...ooer ainen tairmeen baim artst
Which doctor/chemist _____ has night/weekend duty?	Welcher Arzt/welche Apotheke hat Nachtdienst/Notdienst?
	velkher artst/velkher apotayker hat nakht deenst/noat deenst?

13.2 **P**atient's ailments

I don't feel well _____	Ich fühle mich unwohl
	ikh fueler mikh oonvoal
I'm dizzy _____	Mir ist schwindlig
	meer ist shvindlikh
– ill_____	Ich bin krank
	ikh bin krank
– sick_____	Mir ist schlecht/übel
	meer ist shlekht/uebel
I've got a cold_____	Ich bin erkältet
	ikh bin erkelltet
It hurts here _____	Ich habe hier Schmerzen
	ikh harber heer shmertsen
I've been throwing up _____	Ich habe mich übergeben
	ikh harber mikh uebergayben
I've got... _____	Ich habe...Beschwerden
	ikh harber...beshverden
I'm running a _____ temperature of...degrees	Ich habe...(Grad) Fieber
	ikh harber...(grart) feeber
I've been stung by_____ a wasp	Ich bin von einer Wespe gestochen worden
	ikh bin fon ainer vesper geshtokhen vorden
I've been stung by an_____ insect	Ein Insekt hat mich gestochen oder gebissen
	ain inzekt hat mikh geshtokhen oader gebissen
I've been bitten by _____ a dog	Mich hat ein Hund gebissen
	mikh hat ain hoont gebissen
I've been stung by_____ a jellyfish	Mich hat eine Qualle gestochen
	mikh hat ainer kvaller geshtokhen
I've been bitten by _____ a snake	Mich hat eine Schlange gebissen
	mikh hat ainer shlanger gebissen

I've been bitten by _____ an animal	Mich hat ein Tier gebissen *mikh hat ain teer gebissen*
I've cut myself _____	Ich habe mich geschnitten *ikh harber mikh geshnitten*
I've burned myself _____	Ich habe mich verbrannt *ikh harber mikh fayrbrant*
I've grazed myself _____	Ich habe eine Hautabschürfung *ikh harber ainer howt ap shuer foong*
I've had a fall _____	Ich bin gestürzt *ikh bin geshtuertst*
I've sprained my ankle _____	Ich habe mir den Knöchel verstaucht *ikh harber meer den knoekhel fairshtowkht*
I've come for the _____ morning-after pill	Ich möchte die 'Pille danach' *ikh moekhter dee 'piller darnakh'*

13 .3 The consultation

Was für Beschwerden haben Sie? _____ (Wo fehlt's denn?)	What seems to be the problem?
Wie lange haben Sie diese _____ Beschwerden schon?	How long have you had these symptoms?
Haben Sie diese Beschwerden schon _____ früher gehabt?	Have you had this trouble before?
Wie hoch ist das Fieber? _____	How high is your temperature?
Machen Sie sich bitte frei _____	Get undressed, please
Machen Sie bitte den Oberkörper frei _____	Strip to the waist, please
Sie können sich dort _____ ausziehen/freimachen	You can undress there
Bitte machen Sie den linken/rechten _____ Arm frei	Roll up your left/right sleeve, please
Legen Sie sich hierauf _____	Lie down here, please
Tut das weh?/Haben Sie hier _____ Schmerzen?	Does this hurt?
Tief ein- und ausatmen _____	Breathe deeply
Öffnen Sie den Mund _____	Open your mouth

Patient's medical history

I'm a diabetic _____	Ich bin zuckerkrank/Diabetiker *ikh bin tsooker krank/deea bayt ikker*
I have a heart condition _____	Ich bin herzkrank/Ich habe ein Herzleiden *ikh bin hairtskrank/ikh harber ain hertslaiden*
I have asthma _____	Ich habe Asthma/Ich bin Asthmatiker *ikh harber astmar/ikh bin astmartikker*
I'm allergic to... _____	Ich bin allergisch gegen... *ikh bin allairgish gaygen...*
I'm...months pregnant _____	Ich bin...Monate schwanger *ikh bin...moanarter shvanger*
I'm on a diet _____	Ich habe eine Diät *ikh harber ainer deeyayt*
I'm on medication/the pill _____	Ich nehme Medikamente/die Pille *ikh naymer medee ker menter/dee piller*

Sickness

I've had a heart attack _____ once before	Ich habe schon mal einen Herzanfall gehabt
	ikh harber shoan mall ainen hertsanfall gehapt
I've had a(n)...operation ___	Ich bin am/an der...operiert
	ikh bin am/an dayr...opereert
I've been ill recently _____	Ich bin gerade krank gewesen
	ikh bin gerarder krank gevayzen
I've got an ulcer _____	Ich habe ein Magengeschwür
	ikh harber ain margen geshvuer
I've got my period _____	Ich habe meine Periode
	ikh harber mainer peree oader

Sind Sie gegen irgendetwas _____ allergisch?	Do you have any allergies?
Nehmen Sie Medikamente (ein)? _____	Are you on any medication?
Haben Sie eine Diät? _____	Are you on a diet?
Sind Sie schwanger? _____	Are you pregnant?
Sind Sie gegen Wundstarrkrampf _____ geimpft?	Have you had a tetanus injection?

Es ist nichts Ernstes _____	It's nothing serious
Sie haben sich den/die/das... _____ gebrochen	Your...is broken
Sie haben sich den/die/das... _____ verstaucht	You've sprained...
Sie haben einen Riss... _____	You've got (a) torn...
Sie haben eine Entzündung _____	You've got an inflammation
Sie haben Blinddarmentzündung _____	You've got appendicitis
Sie haben Bronchitis _____	You've got bronchitis
Sie haben eine Geschlechtskrankheit _____	You've got a venereal disease
Sie haben Grippe _____	You've got the flu
Sie haben einen Herzanfall gehabt _____	You've had a heart attack
Sie haben eine Infektion (Virus, _____ bakterielle)	You've got an infection (viral, bacterial)
Sie haben Lungenentzündung _____	You've got pneumonia
Sie haben ein Magengeschwür _____	You've got an ulcer
Sie haben eine Muskelzerrung _____	You've pulled a muscle
Sie haben eine vaginale Entzündung _____	You've got a vaginal infection
Sie haben eine _____ Lebensmittelvergiftung/Nahrungs-mittelvergiftung	You've got food poisoning
Sie haben einen Sonnenstich _____	You've got sunstroke
Sie sind allergisch gegen... _____	You're allergic to...
Sie sind schwanger _____	You're pregnant

Sickness

Ich möchte eine_____	I'd like to have your
Blut/Harn/Stuhluntersuchung machen lassen	blood/urine/stools tested
Es muss genäht werden_____	It needs stitching
Ich schicke Sie zu einem Facharzt/ins____ Krankenhaus/Hospital	I'm referring you to a specialist/sending you to hospital.
Es müssen Röntgenaufnahmen gemacht werden _____	You'll need to have some x-rays taken
Setzen Sie sich bitte (wieder) ins_____ Wartezimmer_____	Could you wait in the waiting room, please?
Sie müssen operiert werden_____	You'll need an operation

The diagnosis

Is it contagious?_____	Ist es ansteckend?
	ist ez anshtekkent?
How long do I have to _____ stay...?	Wie lange muss ich...bleiben?
	vee langer mooss ikh...blaiben?
– in bed _____	Wie lange muss ich im Bett bleiben?
	vee langer mooss ikh im bett blaiben?
– in hospital _____	Wie lange muss ich im Krankenhaus bleiben?
	vee langer mooss ikh im kranken howz blaiben?
Do I have to go on _____ a special diet?	Muss ich eine Diät einhalten?
	mooss ikh ainer deeyayt ainhalten?
Am I allowed to travel? ____	Darf ich reisen?
	darf ikh raizen?
Can I make a new _____ appointment?	Kann ich einen neuen Termin machen?
	kan ikh ainen noyen termeen makhen?
When do I have to_____ come back?	Wann soll ich wiederkommen?
	van zoll ikh veeder kommen?
I'll come back _____ tomorrow	Ich komme morgen wieder
	ikh kommer morgen veeder

| Kommen Sie morgen/in ... _____ Tagen wieder | Come back tomorrow/in...days' time. |

.4 Medication and prescriptions

How do I take this _____ medicine?	Wie soll ich diese Medikamente einnehmen?
	vee zoll ikh deezer medee kar menter ain naymen?
How many capsules/ _____ drops/injections/spoon-fuls/tablets each time?	Wieviel Kapseln/Tropfen/Spritzen/Löffel/Tabletten/Zäpfchen pro Mal?
	veefeel kapseln/tropfen/shpritsen/loeffel/ tabletten/tsepfkhen pro marl?
How many times a day? ___	Wie oft täglich?
	vee oft tayglikh?

I've forgotten my _____ medication. At home I take...	Ich habe meine Medikamente vergessen. Zu hause nehme ich...
	ikh harber mainer medee kar menter fairgessen. tsoo howzer naymer ikh...
Could you make out a _____ prescription for me?	Können Sie mir ein Rezept ausstellen?
	koennen zee meer ain retsept ows shtellen?

Ich verschreibe Ihnen ein _____ Antibiotikum/einen Saft/ein Beruhigungsmittel/Schmerzmittel	I'm prescribing antibiotics/a mixture/a tranquilliser/pain killers
Sie dürfen sich nicht anstrengen/Sie ____ müssen sich schonen	Have lots of rest
Sie dürfen nicht nach draussen _____	Stay indoors
Sie müssen im Bett bleiben_____	Stay in bed

alle...Stunden	Kapseln	Spritzen
every...hours	capsules	injections
die Kur beenden	Löffel (Ess-/Tee-)	Tabletten
finish the course	spoonfuls	tablets
dieses Medikament beeinträchtigt die Fahrtüchtigkeit	(tablespoons/ teaspoons)	Tropfen
	...mal täglich	drops
this medication impairs your driving	...times a day	vor jeder Mahlzeit
	nicht zerkauen	before meals
einnehmen	do not chew	während...Tagen
take	nur für äusserliche Anwendung	for...days
einreiben		Zäpfchen
rub on	for external use only	suppository
in Wasser (auf)lösen	Salbe	
dissolve in water	ointment	

.5 At the dentist's

Do you know a good _____ dentist?	Können Sie mir einen guten Zahnarzt/Dentisten empfehlen?
	koennen zee meer ainen gooten tsarn artst/denteesten empfaylen?
Could you make a _____ dentist's appointment for me? It's urgent	Können Sie mir einen Termin beim Zahnarzt besorgen? Es eilt
	koennen zee meer ainen termeen baim tsarn artst bezorgen? Ez ailt
Can I come in today,_____ please?	Könnte ich bitte heute noch kommen?
	koennter ikh bitter hoyter nokh kommen?
I have (terrible)_____ toothache	Ich habe (schreckliche) Zahnschmerzen
	ikh harber (shrek likher) tsarn shmertsen

Sickness

Could you prescribe/ _____ give me a painkiller?	Können Sie mir ein Schmerzmittel verschreiben/geben? *koennen zee meer ain shmairts mittel fairshraiben/gayben?*
A piece of my tooth/_____ molar has broken off	Mir ist ein Stück vom Zahn/Backenzahn abgebrochen *meer ist ain shtuek fom tsarn/bakkentsarn apgebrokhen*
My filling's come out _____	Ich habe eine Füllung verloren *ikh harber ainer fuellung fairloren*
I've got a broken crown_____	Mir ist eine Krone abgebrochen *meer ist ainer kroner apgebrokhen*
I'd like/I don't want a _____ local anaesthetic	Ich möchte (nicht) örtlich betäubt werden *ikh moekhter (nikht) oertlikh betoypt verden*
Can you do a makeshift_____ repair job?	Können Sie mir jetzt provisorisch helfen? *koennen zee meer yetst provee zorish helfen?*
I don't want this tooth _____ pulled	Ich will nicht, dass dieser Zahn gezogen wird *ikh vill nikht, dass deezer tsarn getsoagen virt*
My dentures are broken. _____ Can you fix them?	Mein Gebiss ist zerbrochen. Können Sie es reparieren? *main gebiss ist tsayrbrokhen. koennen zee es repareeren?*

Welcher Zahn/(Backenzahn) tut weh?_____	Which tooth hurts?
Sie haben ein(en) Abszess_____	You've got an abscess
Ich muss eine Nervenbehandlung_____ machen/durchführen	I'll have to do a root canal
Ich betäube Sie örtlich _____	I'm giving you a local anaesthetic
Ich muss diesen..._____ füllen/ziehen/abschleifen	I'll have to fill/pull/file this tooth
Ich muss bohren_____	I'll have to drill
Mund auf, bitte _____	Open wide, please
Mund zu,bitte_____	Close your mouth, please

Sickness

107

In trouble

14 In trouble

14.1 Asking for help

Help! _____	Hilfe!
	hillfer!
Fire! _____	Feuer!
	foyer!
Police! _____	Polizei!
	poleetsai!
Quick! _____	Schnell!
	shnell!
Danger! _____	Gefahr!
	gefahr!
Watch out! _____	Achtung!
	akhtoong!
Stop! _____	Halt!
	halt!
Be careful! _____	Vorsicht!
	forzikht!
Don't! _____	Nicht tun!
	nikht toon!
Let go! _____	Loslassen!
	loaslassen!
Stop that thief! _____	Halten den Dieb!
	haltet den deep!
Could you help me, _____ please?	Würden Sie mir bitte helfen?
	vuerden zee meer bitter helfen?
Where's the police _____ station/emergency exit/fire escape?	Wo ist die Polizeiwache/der Notausgang/die Feuertreppe?
	vo ist dee polee tsai vakher/der noat ows gang/dee foyer trepper?
Where's the fire _____ extinguisher?	Wo ist ein Feuerlöscher?
	vo ist ain foyer loesher?
Call the fire brigade! _____	Rufen Sie die Feuerwehr!
	roofen zee dee foyer vair!
Call the police! _____	Rufen Sie die Polizei (an)
	roofen zee dee poleetsai (an)
Call an ambulance! _____	Rufen Sie einen Krankenwagen/Rettungswagen
	roofen zee ainen krunken vargen/rettoongs vargen
Where's the nearest _____ phone?	Wo gibt's ein Telefon?
	vo gipt's ain telefoan?
Could I use your phone? ___	Darf ich Ihr Telefon benutzen?
	darf ikh eer telefoan benootsen?
What's the emergency _____ number?	Wie lautet die Alarmnummer?
	vee lowtet dee alarm noomer?
What's the number for _____ the police?	Wie ist die Telefonnummer der Polizei?
	vee ist dee telefoan noomer dayr poleetsai?

14 .2 Loss

I've lost my purse/_____ wallet	Ich habe mein Portemonnaie/meine Brieftasche verloren *ikh harber main portmonnay/mainer breeftasher fairloren*
I left my...yesterday _____	Ich habe gestern mein(en)/meine... vergessen *ikh harber gestern main(en)/mainer... fairgessen*
I left my...here _____	Ich habe hier mein(en)/meine... liegengelassen/stehengelassen *ikh harber heer main(en)/mainer...leegen gelassen/shtayen gelassen*
Did you find my...? _____	Haben Sie mein(en)/meine...gefunden? *harben zee main(en)/mainer...gefoonden?*
It was right here_____	Er/sie/es stand/lag hier *er/zee/es shtant/lark heer*
It's quite valuable _____	Es ist sehr wertvoll *ez ist zayr vayrtfoll*
Where's the lost_____ property office?	Wo ist das Fundbüro? *vo ist dass funt buero?*

14 .3 Accidents

There's been an accident __	Es ist ein Unfall passiert *ez ist ain unfarl passeert*
Someone's fallen into _____ the water	Jemand ist ins Wasser gefallen *yaymant ist ins vasser gefallen*
There's a fire_____	Es brennt *ez brennt*
Is anyone hurt? _____	Ist jemand verletzt? *ist yaymant fairletst?*
Some people have _____ been/no one's been injured	Es gibt (keine) Verletzte(n) *ez gipt (kainer) fairletste(n)*
There's someone in _____ the car/train still	Es ist noch jemand im Auto/Zug *ez ist nokh yaymant im owto/tsook*
It's not too bad. Don't_____ worry	Es ist nicht so schlimm. Machen Sie sich keine Sorgen *ez ist nikht zo shlimm. makhen zee zikh kainer zorgen*
Leave everything the _____ way it is, please	Lassen Sie bitte alles, so wie es ist *lassen zee bitter alles, zo vee ez ist*
I want to talk to the_____ police first	Ich will erst mit der Polizei sprechen *ikh vill airst mit dayr poleetsai shprekhen*
I want to take a _____ photo first	Ich will erst ein Foto machen *ikh vill airst ain foto makhen*
Here's my name_____ and address	Hier sind mein Name und meine Adresse *heer zint main narmer unt mainer adresser*
Could I have your _____ name and address?	Geben Sie mir bitte Ihren Namen und Ihre Adresse *gayben zee meer bitter eeren narmen unt eerer adresser*

In trouble

Could I see some _____ identification/your insurance papers?	Dürfte ich Ihren Ausweis/Ihre Versicherungspapiere sehen? *duerfter ikh eeren owsvais/eerer fairzikheroongs papeerer zayhen?*
Will you act as a _____ witness?	Wollen Sie Zeuge sein? *vollen zee tsoyger zain?*
I need the details for _____ the insurance	Ich brauche die Angaben für die Versicherung *ikh browkher dee angarben fuer dee fair zikhe roong*
Are you insured? _____	Sind Sie versichert? *zint zee fairzikhert?*
Third party or _____ comprehensive?	Haftpflicht oder Vollkasko-Versicherung? *haftpflikht oader follkassko-fairzikhe roong?*
Could you sign here, _____ please?	Unterschreiben Sie hier bitte *oonter shraiben zee heer bitter*

14 .4 Theft

I've been robbed _____	Ich bin bestohlen worden *ikh bin beshtoalen vorden*
My...has been stolen _____	Mein(e) ... ist gestohlen worden *main(er) ... ist geshtoalen vorden*
My car's been _____ broken into	Mein Auto ist aufgebrochen worden *main owto ist owfgebrokhen vorden*

14 .5 Missing person

I've lost my child/ _____ grandmother	Mein Kind/meine Oma ist verschwunden *main kint/mainer oamar ist fairshvoonden*
Could you help me _____ find him/her?	Würden Sie mir bitte suchen helfen? *vuerden zee meer bitter zookhen helfen?*
Have you seen a _____ small child?	Haben Sie ein kleines Kind gesehen? *harben zee ain klaines kint gezayhen?*
He's/she's...years old _____	Er/sie ist...Jahre *er/zee ist...yahrer*
He's/she's got short/long/blond/red/ brown/black/grey/curly/ straight/frizzy hair	Er/sie hat kurzes/langes/blondes/rotes/braunes/ schwarzes/graues/lockiges/glattes/gekräu seltes Haar *er/zee hat koortses/langes/blondes/roates/ brownes/shvartses/growes/lokigges/glattes/ gekroyzeltes har*
with a ponytail _____	mit Pferdeschwanz *mit pferder shvants*
with plaits _____	mit Zöpfen *mit tsoepfen*
in a bun _____	mit einem Knoten/Dutt *mit ainem knooten/doott*
He's/she's got _____ blue/brown/green eyes	Die Augen sind blau/braun/grün *dee owgen zint blow/brown/gruen*
He's wearing swimming _____ trunks/mountaineering boots	Er trägt eine Badehose/Wanderschuhe *er traykht ainer barder hoazer/vander shooer*

In trouble

14.

with/without glasses/	mit/ohne Brille
	mit/oaner briller
tall/short	gross/klein
	groass/klain
This is a photo of	Hier ist ein Bild von ihm/ihr
him/her	*heer ist ain bilt fon eem/eer*
He/she must be lost	Er/sie hat sich sicher verlaufen
	er/zee hat zikh zikher fairlowfen

.6 The police

An arrest

Ihre Fahrzeugpapiere bitte	Your registration papers, please
Sie sind zu schnell gefahren	You were speeding
Sie parken falsch	You're not allowed to park here
Sie haben kein Geld in die Parkuhr gesteckt	You haven't put money in the meter
Ihr Licht brennt nicht	Your lights aren't working
Sie bekommen eine gebühren-pflichtige Verwarnung/einen Strafzettel von...	You are to receive a fine of/a parking ticket for...
Zahlen Sie sofort?	Do you want to pay on the spot?
Sie müssen sofort bezahlen	You'll have to pay on the spot

I don't speak German	Ich spreche kein Deutsch
	ikh shprekher kain doytsh
I didn't see the sign	Ich habe das Schild nicht gesehen
	ikh harber das shilt nikht gezayhen
I don't understand what it says	Ich verstehe nicht, was da steht
	ikh fairshtayher nikht, vass dar shtayt
I was only doing... kilometres an hour	Ich bin nur...Kilometer pro Stunde gefahren
	ikh bin noor...keelomayter pro shtoonder gefahren
I'll have my car checked	Ich werde mein Auto nachsehen lassen
	ikh verder main owto nakh zayhen lassen
I was blinded by oncoming lights	Der Gegenverkehr hat mich geblendet
	dayr gaygen fairkair hat mikh geblendet

In trouble

At the police station

Wo ist es passiert? _____	Where did it happen?
Was haben Sie verloren? _____	What's missing?
Was ist gestohlen (worden)?_____	What's been taken?
Ihren Ausweis bitte _____	Could I see some identification?
Wann ist es passiert? _____	What time did it happen?
Wer war daran beteiligt? _____	Who was involved?
Gibt es Zeugen? _____	Are there any witnesses?
Bitte füllen Sie das aus_____	Fill this out, please
Hier bitte unterschreiben _____	Sign here, please
Möchten Sie einen Dolmetscher? ___	Do you want an interpreter?

I want to report a_____ collision/something missing/rape/missing person	Ich möchte einen Zusammenstoss/einen (things missing)Verlust/eine Vergewaltigung anzeigen/(persons missing) Ich möchte eine Vermisstenanzeige machen
	ikh moekhter ainen tsoo zammen shtoas/ainen fairloost/ainer fair gevalti goong an tsaigen/ikh moekhter ainer fayrmissten antsaiger makhen
Could you make out _____ a report, please?	Würden Sie bitte ein Protokoll aufnehmen?
	vuerden zee bitter ain proatoakoll owfnaymen?
Could I have a copy _____ for the insurance?	Geben Sie mir bitte eine Abschrift für die Versicherung
	gayben zee meer bitter ainer apshrift fuer dee fair zeekhe roong
I've lost everything _____	Ich habe alles verloren
	ikh harber alles fairloren
All my money is gone, I don't know what to do ___	Mein Geld ist alle, ich bin ratlos
	main gelt ist aller, ikh bin rartloas
Could you please lend me some?	Könnten Sie mir bitte etwas leihen?
	koennten zee meer bitter etvass laihen?
I'd like an interpreter _____	Ich möchte einen Dolmetscher
	ikh moekhter ainen dolmetsher
I'm innocent _____	Ich bin unschuldig
	ikh bin oonshuldikh
I don't know anything _____ about it	Ich weiss von nichts
	ikh vaiss fon nikhts
I want to speak to _____ someone from the British consulate	Ich möchte jemanden vom britischen Konsulat sprechen
	ikh moekhter yaymanden fom breetishen konsoolart shprekhen
I need to see someone ___ from the British embassy	Ich möchte jemanden von der breetischen Botschaft sprechen
	ikh moekhter yaymunden fon dayr britishen boatshaft shprekhen
I want a lawyer who_____ speaks...	Ich will einen Rechtsanwalt, der...spricht
	ikh vill ainen rekhts anvalt, dayr...shprikht

In trouble

113

15

Word list

Word list English - German

● **This word list** is meant to supplement the previous chapters. Nouns are always accompanied by the German definite article in order to indicate whether it is a masculine (*der*), feminine (*die*), or a neuter (*das*), word. In a number of cases, words not contained in this list can be found elsewhere in this book, namely alongside the diagrams of the car, the bicycle and the tent. Many food terms can be found in the German-English list in Section 4.7.

A

about	ungefähr	*oongefayr*
above	über	*ueber*
abroad	das Ausland	*dass owslant*
accident	der Unfall	*dayr oonfarl*
adder	die Natter	*dee natter*
addition	die Addition	*dee adittseeyoan*
address	die Adresse	*dee adresser*
admission	der Eintritt	*dayr aintritt*
admission price	der Eintrittspreis	*dayr aintritts praiss*
advice	der Rat	*dayr rart*
after	nach	*nakh*
afternoon	mittags	*mittargs*
aftershave	die After-shave-Lotion	*dee after-shave loatseeyown*
again	erneut	*ayrnoyt*
against	gegen	*gaygen*
age	das Alter	*dass alter*
Aids	(das) Aids	*(dass) aids*
air conditioning	die Klimaanlage	*dee kleemar anlarger*
air mattress	die Luftmatratze	*dee looft mattratser*
air sickness bag	die Spucktüte	*dee shpook tueter*
aircraft	das Flugzeug	*dass flooktsoyk*
airport	der Flughafen	*dayr flookharfen*
alarm	der Alarm	*dayr alarm*
alarm clock	der Wecker	*dayr vekker*
alcohol	der Alkohol	*dayr alkohol*
allergic	allergisch	*allayrgish*
alone	allein	*allain*
always	immer	*immer*
ambulance	der Rettungswagen	*dayr rettoongs vargen*
amount	der Betrag	*dayr betrarg*
amusement park	der Vergnügungspark	*dayr fayr gnue goongs park*
anchovy	die Anschovis	*dee antshoveez*
and	und	*oont*
angry	böse	*boezer*
animal	das Tier	*dass teer*
ankle	der Knöchel	*dayr knoekhel*
answer	die Antwort	*dee antvort*
ant	die Ameise	*dee armaizer*
antibiotics	das Antibiotikum	*dass antee beeotee kum*
antifreeze	das Frostschutzmittel	*dass frost shoots mittel*

antique	alt/(books) antiquarisch	alt/ anteekvarish
antiques	die Antiquität	dee antee kveetayt
anus	der After	dayr after
apartment	das Appartement	dass appartamong
aperitif	der Aperitif	dayr appereeteef
apologies	die Entschuldigung	dee ent shooldigoong
apple	der Apfel	dayr apfel
apple juice	der Apfelsaft	dayr apfelzaft
apple pie	der Apfelkuchen	dayr apfel kookhen
apple sauce	das Apfelmus	dass apfel moos
appointment	der Termin	dayr termeen
apricot	die Aprikose	dee apree koazer
	(Aus.) die Marille	dee Mariller
April	der April	dayr aprill
Archbishop	der Erzbischof	dayr airts bishoaf
architecture	die Architektur	dee arkhee tektoor
area	die Umgebung	dee oom gay boong
arena	die Manege	dee manerjer
arm	der Arm	dayr arm
arrange	(sich) verabreden	(sikh) fayr aprayden
arrive	ankommen	ankommen
arrow	der Pfeil	dayr pfail
art	die Kunst	dee koonst
artery	die Schlagader	dee shlarkarder
artichokes	die Artischocke	dee artee shokker
article	der Artikel	dayr arteekel
artificial respiration	die künstliche Beatmung	dee kuenstlikher beart moong
ashtray	der Aschenbecher	dayr ashenbekher
ask	fragen	frargen
ask for	bitten um	bitten oom
asparagus	der Spargel	dayr shpargel
aspirin	das Aspirin	dass asspireen
assault	die Vergewaltigung	dee fayr gevaltee goong
at home	zu Hause	tsoo howzer
at the front	vorn	forn
at the latest	spätestens	shpaytestenz
aubergine	die Aubergine	dee owberjeener
August	der August	dayr owgoost
automatic	automatisch	owtow mar teesh
autumn	der Herbst	dayr hayrpst
avalanche	die Lawine	dee laveener
awake	wach	varkh
awning	das Vordach	dass fordakh

B

baby	das Baby	dass baybee
baby food	die Babynahrung	dee baybee nahroong
babysitter	der Babysitter	dayr baybee zitter
back (at the)	hinten	hinten
back	der Rücken	dayr ruekken
bacon	der Speck	dayr shpek
bad	schlecht/schlimm	shlekht/shlim
bag	die Tasche	dee tasher
bakery	der Bäckerei	dee bekerai
balcony	der Balkon	dayr balkoan

ball	der Ball	*dayr barl*
ballet	das Ballett	*dass balett*
ballpoint pen	der Kugelschreiber/	*dayr koogel shraiber/*
	der Kuli	*dayr koolee*
banana	die Banane	*dee banarner*
bandage	der Verband	*dayr fayrbant*
bank (river)	das Ufer	*dass oofer*
bank	die Bank	*dee bank*
bank pass	die Scheckkarte	*dee shekkarter*
bar	die Bar	*dee bar*
barbecue	das Barbecue	*dass barbekyu*
basketball (to play)	das Baskettballspiel	*dass basket barl shpeel*
bath	das Bad	*dass bart*
bath attendant	der Bademeister	*dayr barder maister*
bath foam	das Schaumbad	*dass showmbart*
bath towel	das Handtuch/(large)	*dass hanttookh/*
	das Badelaken	*dass barder larken*
bathing cap	die Badekappe	*dee barder kapper*
bathing cubicle	die Badekabine	*dee barder kabeener*
bathing suit	der Badeanzug	*dayr barder antsook*
bathroom	das Badezimmer	*dass barder tsimmer*
battery	die Batterie	*dee batteree*
be in love with	verliebt sein in	*fayrleept zain in*
beach	der Strand	*dayr shtrant*
beans	die Bohnen	*dee boanen*
beautiful	schön/prächtig	*shoen/prekhtikh*
beauty parlour	der Kosmetiksalon	*dayr kozmaytik zalong*
bed	das Bett	*dass bett*
bee	die Biene	*dee beener*
beef	das Rindfleisch	*dass rintflaish*
beer	das Bier	*dass beer*
beetroot	die rote Bete	*dee roater bayter*
begin	anfangen/beginnen	*anfangen/beginnen*
beginner	der Anfänger	*dayr anfenger*
behind	(prep.) hinter/	*hinter/*
	(adj.) hinten	*hinten*
Belgian	der Belgier/	*dayr bellgiyer/*
	die Belgierin	*dee bellgiyerin*
Belgium	Belgien	*bellgiyen*
belt	der Gürtel	*dayr guertel*
berth	der Liegeplatz	*dayr leeger plats*
better	besser	*besser*
bicycle	das Fahrrad	*dass far rart*
bicycle pump	die Luftpumpe	*dee looft poomper*
	(fürs Fahrrad)	*(fuers far rart)*
bicycle repairman	der Fahrradhändler	*dayr farrart hendler*
bikini	der Bikini	*dayr bikeeni*
bill	die Rechnung	*dee rekhnoong*
billiards (to play)	Billard spielen	*billyard shpeelen*
birthday	der Geburtstag	*dayr geboorts tark*
biscuit	der Biskuit/der Keks	*dayr biskveet/keks*
bite (to)	beissen	*baissen*
bitter	bitter	*bitter*
black	schwarz	*shvarts*
bland	geschmacklos	*geshmakkloass*
blanket	die Decke	*dee dekker*
bleach	blondieren	*blondeeren*

Word list

15

117

blister	die Blase	*dee blarzer*
blond	blond	*blont*
blood	das Blut	*dass bloot*
blood pressure	der Blutdruck	*dayr bloot drook*
blouse	die Bluse	*dee bloozer*
blow dry	föhnen	*foenen*
blue	blau	*blow*
board (on)	an Bord	*an bort*
boat	das Boot	*dass boat*
body	der Körper	*dayr koerper*
body milk	die Bodylotion	*dee body loa tseeoan*
boiled	gekocht	*gekokht*
bonbon	die Praline/	*dee praleener/*
	das Bonbon	*dass bonbon*
bone	der Knochen	*dayr knokhen*
bonnet	die Motorhaube	*dee moator howber*
book (to)	reservieren	*rezayrveeren*
book	das Buch	*dass bookh*
booked	reserviert	*rezayrveert*
booking office	die Vorverkaufsstelle	*dee for fayrkowfs shteller*
bookshop	die Buchhandlung	*dee bookh hand loong*
border	die Grenze	*dee grentser*
bored (to be)	sich langweilen	*zikh langvailen*
boring	langweilig	*langvailikh*
born	geboren	*geboren*
borrow	ausleihen	*owslaihen*
botanical gardens	der Botanische Garten	*dayr boatarnisher garten*
both	beides	*baidez*
bottle	die Flasche	*dee flasher*
bottle-warmer	der Flaschenwärmer	*dayr flashen vermer*
box	der Karton	*dayr karton*
box	die Loge	*dee loajer*
boy	der Junge	*dayr yoonger*
bra	der BH	*dayr bayhar*
bracelet	das Armband	*dass armbant*
braised	gedünstet/gesotten	*geduenstet/gezotten*
brake	die Bremse	*dee bremzer*
brake fluid	die Bremsflüssigkeit	*dee bremz fluessikh kait*
brake oil	das Bremsöl	*dass bremzoel*
bread	das Brot	*dass broat*
break	(zer-)brechen	*(tsair-)brekhen*
breakfast	das Frühstück	*dass frueshtuek*
breast	die Brust	*dee broost*
bridge	die Brücke	*dee brueker*
briefs	der Schlüpfer	*dayr shluepfer*
bring	(mit-)bringen	*(mit-)bringen*
brochure	die Broschüre	*dee broashuerer*
broken	kaputt	*kapoott*
brother	der Bruder	*dayr brooder*
brown	braun	*brown*
brush	die Bürste	*dee buerster*
Brussels sprouts	der Rosenkohl	*dayr rozenkoal*
bucket	der Eimer	*dayr aimer*
bug	das Ungeziefer	*dass oon getseefer*
building	das Gebäude	*dass geboyder*

buoy	die Boje	*dee boayer*
burglary	der Einbruch	*dayr ainbrookh*
burn	verbrennen	*fair brennen*
burnt	angebrannt	*angebrant*
bus	der (Auto-)Bus	*dayr (owtoa-) booss*
bus station	der Busbahnhof	*dayr booss barnhoaf*
bus stop	die Bushaltestelle	*dee booss halter shteller*
business class	Business Class	*bizniss klarss*
business trip	die Geschäftsreise	*dee geshefts raizer*
busy	lebhaft/geschäftig	*layphaft/gesheftikh*
butane camping gas	das Butangas	*dass bootarn gass*
butcher	der Schlachter/	*dayr shlakhter/*
	der Metzger	*dayr mettsger*
butter	die Butter	*dee bootter*
button	der Knopf	*dayr knopf*
buy	kaufen	*kowfen*
by airmail	per Luftpost	*payr looftpost*

C

cabbage	der Kohl	*dayr koal*
cabin	die Kabine	*dee kabeener*
cake	der Kuchen/	*dayr kukhen/*
	das (Stück) Gebäck	*dass (shtuek) gebeck*
cake	die Torte	*dee torter*
cake shop	die Konditorei	*dee kondeetorai*
call	anrufen	*anroofen*
called (to be)	heissen	*haissen*
camera	die Kamera	*dee kammerar*
camp	campen	*kampen*
camp shop	der Campingladen	*dayr kamping larden*
camp site	der Campingplatz	*dayr kamping plats*
camper	das Wohnmobil	*dass voan moabeel*
campfire	das Lagerfeuer	*dass larger foyer*
camping guide	der Campingführer	*dayr kamping fuerer*
camping permit	die Camping-erlaubnis	*dee kamping ayrlowpniss*
cancel (to)	annullieren	*annooleeren*
candle	die Kerze	*dee kayrtser*
canoe (to)	Kanu fahren	*kanoo faren*
canoe	das Kanu	*dass kanoo*
car	das Auto	*dass owtoa*
car	der Waggon	*dayr vaggorn*
car deck	das Autodeck	*dass owtoa deck*
car documents	die Fahrzeugpapiere	*dee far tsoyk papeerer*
car park (multi-storey)	die Parkgarage	*dee parkgararjer*
car seat	der Kindersitz	*dayr kinderzits*
car trouble	die Panne	*dee panner*
carafe	die Karaffe	*dee karaffer*
caravan	der Wohnwagen	*dayr voan vargen*
cardigan	die Jacke	*dee yakker*
careful	vorsichtig	*forzikhtikh*
carrot	die Karotte	*dee karotter*
carton of cigarettes	die Stange Zigaretten	*dee shtanger tsigaretten*
cascade	der Wasserfall	*dayr vasserfall*
cash desk	die Kasse	*dee kasser*

casino	das Kasino	dass kasseeno
cassette	die Cassette	dee kassetter
castle	das Schloss	dass shloss
cat	die Katze	dee kattser
catalogue	der Katalog	dayr kataloag
cathedral	die Kathedrale	dee kattee drarler
cauliflower	der Blumenkohl (S.Ger.,Aus.) der Karfiol	dayr bloomen koal dayr karfeeol
cave	die Höhle	dee hoehler
CD	die CD	dee tsaydee
celebrate	feiern	faiern
cellotape	das Klebeband	dass klayberbant
cemetery	der Friedhof	dayr freethoaf
centimetre	der/das Zentimeter	dayr/dass tsen tee mayter
central heating	die Zentralheizung	dee tsentrarl hai tsoong
centre	die Mitte	dee mitter
centre	das Zentrum	dass tsen troom
chair	der Stuhl	dayr shtool
chambermaid	das Zimmermädchen	dass tsimmer maydkhen
champagne	der Champagner/Sekt	dayr shampanyer/zekt
change (alter)	ändern	endern
change (one thing for another)	wechseln	vekhseln
change (trains)	umsteigen	oomshtaigen
change the baby's nappy	wickeln	vikkeln
chapel	die Kapelle	dee kappeller
charter flight	der Charterflug	dayr charter flook
chat up	jemand anmachen/ sich jemand angeln	yaymant anmakhen/ zikh yaymant angeln
check	kontrollieren	kontrolleeren
check in	sich anmelden	zikh anmelden
cheers	Prost/zum Wohl	prost/tsoom voal
cheese (mature, mild)	der Käse (alte, junge)	dayr kayzer (alter, yoonger)
chef	der Chef	dayr shef
chemist	die Drogerie	dee drogeree
cheque	der Scheck	dayr shek
cherries	Kirschen	dee keershen
chess	das Schachspiel	dass shakhshpeel
chewing gum	der/das Kaugummi	dayr/dass kowgoomee
chicken	das Huhn/Hühnchen/ Hähnchen	dass hoon/huenkhen/ haynkhen
chicory	der Chicorée	dayr chikoree
child	das Kind	dass kint
child's seat	der Kindersitz	dayr kinderzits
chilled	gekühlt	gekuehlt
chin	das Kinn	dass kinn
chips	Pommes frites	pomm frits
chocolate	die Schokolade	dee shoko larder
choose	wählen	vaylen
chop	das Kotelett	dass kotlayt
christian name	der Vorname	dayr fornarmer
church	die Kirche	dee keerkher

church service	der Gottesdienst	*dayr gottes deenst*
cigar	die Zigarre	*dee tseegarrer*
cigar shop	der Tabakladen	*dayr tarbak larden/*
cigarette	die Zigarette	*dee tseegaretter*
cigarette paper	das Zigarettenpapier	*dass tseegaretten papeer*
ciné camera	die Filmkamera	*dee film kamerar*
circle	der Kreis	*dayr krais*
circus	der Zirkus	*dayr tseerkooss*
city map	der Stadtplan	*dayr shtatplarn*
classical concert	das Klassikkonzert	*dass klasseek kontsert*
clean	saubermachen	*zowber makhen*
clean	sauber	*zowber*
clear	deutlich	*doytlikh*
clearance	der Ausverkauf	*dayr owsfairkowf*
clock	die Uhr	*dee ooer*
closed	geschlossen	*geshlossen*
closed off	gesperrt	*geshpayrrt*
clothes	die Kleider	*dee klaider*
clothes hanger	der Kleiderbügel	*dayr klaider buegel*
clothes peg	die Wäscheklammer	*dee vesher klammer*
clothing (piece of)	das Kleidungsstück	*dass klaidoongs shtook*
clothing	die Kleidung	*dee klaidoong*
coach	der Reisebus	*dayr raizerbooss*
coat	der Mantel	*dayr mantel*
cockroach	der Kakerlak	*dayr karkerlak*
cocoa	der Kakao	*dayr kakow*
cod	der Kabeljau	*dayr karbelyow*
coffee	der Kaffee	*dayr kaffay*
coffee filter	der Kaffeefilter	*dayr kaffay filter*
cognac	der Kognak	*dayr konyak*
cold	kalt	*kalt*
cold (a)	die Erkältung	*dee ayrkeltoong*
cold cuts	der Aufschnitt	*dayr owfshnit*
collarbone	das Schlüsselbein	*dass shluessel bain*
colleague	der Kollege	*dayr kolleger*
collision	der Zusammenstoss	*dayr tsoo zammen shtoas*
cologne	das Eau de toilette	*dass oadetwalet*
colour	die Farbe	*dee farber*
colour pencils	die Buntstifte	*dee boont shtifter*
colour TV	der Farbfernseher	*dayr farp fayrn zayer*
colouring book	das Malbuch	*dass marlbookh*
comb	der Kamm	*dayr kamm*
come	kommen	*kommen*
come back	zurückkommen	*tsooruek kommen*
compartment	das Abteil	*dass aptail*
complaint (physical)	das Leiden	*dass laiden*
complaint	die Beschwerde/	*dee beshverder/*
	die Beanstandung	*dee bean shtan doong*
complaints book	das Beschwerdebuch	*dass beshvayrder bookh*
completely	ganz	*gants*
compliment	das Kompliment	*dass kompleement*
compulsory	verpflichtet	*fayrpflikhtet*
concert	das Konzert	*dass kontsayrt*

concert hall	die Konzerthalle	*dee kontsayrt haller*
concussion	die Gehirn-erschütterung	*dee geheern ayr shuete roong*
condensed milk	die Kaffeemilch/die Kondensmilch	*dee kaffay milkh/dee kondens milkh*
condom	das Kondom/der Pariser/das Gummi	*dass kondoam/dayr pareeser/dass goommee*
congratulate	gratulieren	*gratoo leeren*
connection	die Verbindung	*dee fayr bin doong*
constipation	die Verstopfung	*dee fayr shtop foong*
consulate	das Konsulat	*dass konsoolart*
consultation	die Konsultation	*dee kon sool tat tseeoan*
contact lens	die Kontaktlinse	*dee kontakt linzer*
contact lens solution	das Kontaktlinsen-mittel	*dass kontakt linzen mittel*
contagious	ansteckend	*anshtekent*
contraceptive	das Verhütungsmittel	*dass fayr hue toongs mittel*
contraceptive pill	die Verhütungspille	*dee fayr hue toongs piller*
cook (verb)	kochen	*kokhen*
cook	der Koch	*dayr kokh*
copper	das Kupfer	*dass koopfer*
copy	die Kopie	*dee kopee*
corkscrew	der Korkenzieher	*dayr korken tseeher*
corn flour	das Maizena	*dass maitsenar*
corner	die Ecke	*dee ekker*
correct	korrekt	*korrekt*
correspond	korrespondieren	*korrespondeeren*
corridor	der Flur	*dayr flooer*
costume	der Anzug	*dayr antsook*
cot	das Kinderbett	*dass kinderbett*
cotton	die Baumwolle	*dee bowmvoller*
cotton wool	die Watte	*dee vatter*
cough	der Husten	*dayr hoosten*
cough mixture	der Hustensaft	*dayr hoostenzaft*
counter	der Schalter	*dayr shalter*
country	das Land	*dass lant*
country code	die Ländernummer	*dee lender noommer*
courgette	die Zucchini	*dee tsookeenee*
course	(med.) die Kur	*dee koor*
cousin	(m)der Cousin/(f)die Cousine	*dayr koozeen/dee koozeener*
crab	die Krabbe	*dee krabber*
cream	die Creme	*dee kraymer*
cream (for cooking)	die Sahne/der Rahm/	*dee zarner/dayr rarm*
credit card	die Kreditkarte	*dee kredeet karter*
crisps	die Chips	*dee chips*
croissant	das Croissant/das Hörnchen	*dass krwassan/dass hoernshen*
cross (the road)	überqueren	*ueber kvayren*
crossing	die Überfahrt	*dee ueberfart*
cry	weinen	*vainen*
cubic metre	der/das Kubikmeter	*dayr/dass koobeek mayter*

cucumber	die (Salat)gurke	dee (zalart)goorker
cuddly toy	das Kuscheltier	dass kooshelteer
cuff links	die Manschetten knöpfe	dee man shetten knoepfer
cup	die Tasse	dee tasser
	(Aus.) die Schale	dee sharler
curly	lockig	lokikh
current	die Strömung	dee shtroemoong
cushion	das Kissen	dass kissen
customary	üblich	ueblikh
customs	der Zoll/die Zoll-kontrolle	dayr tsoll/dee tsol-kontroller
cut	schneiden	shnaiden
cutlery	das Besteck	dass beshtek
cycle	fahrradfahren	far-rart fahren

D

daily	jeden Tag	yayden tark
dairy products	Molkereiprodukte	molkerai prodookter
damaged	beschädigt	beshaydikt
dance	tanzen	tantsen
danger	die Gefahr	dee gefar
dangerous	gefährlich	gefayrlikh
dark	dunkel	doonkel
date	die Verabredung	dee fayr ap ray doong
daughter	die Tochter	dee tokhter
day	der Tag	dayr tark
day before yesterday	vorgestern	forgestern
dead	tot	toat
decaffeinated	koffeinfrei	koffayeen frai
December	der Dezember	dayr detsember
deck chair	der Strandstuhl/ Strandkorb	dayr shtrantshtool/ dayr shtrantkorp
declare (customs)	verzollen	fayrtsollen
deep	tief	teef
deepfreeze	einfrieren	ainfreeren
degrees	Grad	grart
delay	die Verspätung	dee fayrshpaytoong
delicious	vorzüglich	fortsueglikh
dentist	der Zahnarzt/ der Dentist	dayr tsarnartst/ der denteest
dentures	das Kunstgebiss	dass koonstgebiss
deodorant	das Deo(dorant)	dass deo(dorant)
department	die Abteilung	dee aptailoong
department store	das Kaufhaus	dass kowfhows
departure	die Abfahrt/(flight) der Abflug	dee apfahrt/ dayr apflook
departure time	die Abfahrtszeit	dee apfahrts tsait
depilatory cream	die Enthaarungs creme	dee ent hahroongs kraymer
deposit (to)	zur Aufbewahrung (geben)	tsoor owf bevaroong (gayben)
deposit	die Kaution	dee kowtseeoan
dessert	die Nachspeise	dee nakhshpaizer
destination	das (End)ziel	dass (ent)tseel
destination (mail)	der Bestimmungsort	dayr be shtimoongs ort

develop	entwickeln	*entvikkeln*
diabetic	(m.) der Diabetiker/	*dayr deearbayteeker/*
	(f.) die Diabetikerin	*dee deearbayteekerin*
dial	wählen	*vaylen*
diamond	der Diamant	*dayr deearmant*
diarrhoea	der Durchfall	*dayr doorkhfall*
dictionary	das Wörterbuch	*dass voerter bookh*
diesel	der Diesel	*dayr deezel*
diet	die Diät	*dee deeyayt*
difficulty	die Schwierigkeit	*dee shveerikh kait*
dining room	der Speisesaal	*dayr shpaizerzaal*
dining/buffet car	der Speisewagen	*dayr shpaizer vargen*
dinner (to have)	zu Abend essen	*tsoo arbent essen*
dinner	das Abendessen	*dass arbentessen*
dinner jacket	der Smoking	*dayr smoking*
direction	die Richtung	*dee rikhtoong*
directly	direkt	*deerekt*
dirty	schmierig/schmutzig	*shmeerikh/shmootsikh*
disabled	der/die Behin-	*dayr/dee behin*
	derte	*dayrter*
disco	die Disko	*dee disko*
discount	die Ermässigung/	*dee ermaysi goong/*
	der Nachlass	*dayr nakhlass*
dish	das Gericht	*dass gerikht*
dish of the day	das Tagesgericht	*dass targes gerikht*
disinfectant	das Desinfektions-	*dass dez infektseey*
	mittel	*oanzmittel*
distance	die Entfernung	*dee entfayr noong*
distilled water	das destillierte	*dass destileerter*
	Wasser	*vasser*
disturb	stören	*shtoeren*
disturbance	die Störung	*dee shtoeroong*
dive	tauchen	*towkhen*
diving	der Tauchsport	*dayr towkhshport*
diving (deep sea)	das Tiefseetauchen	*dass teefzaytowkhen*
diving board	das Sprungbrett	*dass shproongbret*
diving gear	die Taucher-	*dee towkher*
	ausrüstung	*owsruestoong*
divorced	geschieden	*gesheeden*
DIY-shop	der Heimwerkermarkt	*dayr haim vayrker markt*
dizzy	schwind(e)lig	*shvind(e)likh*
do	tun	*toon*
doctor	der Arzt/(lady)	*dayr artst/*
	die Ärztin	*dee ayrtstin*
dog	der Hund	*dayr hoont*
doll	die Puppe	*dee pupper*
domestic	das Inland	*dass inlant*
done (cooked)	gar	*gar*
door	die Tür	*dee tuer*
double	Doppel-	*doppel-*
down	unten	*oonten*
draught	der Zug	*dayr tsook*
draughts	das Damespiel	*dass darmeshpeel*
dream	träumen	*troymen*
dress	das Kleid	*dass klait*
dressing gown	der Morgenmantel	*dayr morgen mantel*
drink	trinken	*trinken*

drinking water	das Trinkwasser	dass trinkvasser
drive	fahren	faren
driver	der Fahrer	dayr farer
driving licence	der Führerschein	dayr fuerershain
drought	die Trockenheit	dee trokkenhait
dry	trocknen	trokknen
dry	trocken	trokken
dry clean	reinigen	rainigen
dry cleaner's	die Reinigung	dee rainigoong
dry shampoo	das Pudershampoo/	dass pooder shampoo/
	das Trockenshampoo	dass trokken shampoo
dummy	der Schnuller	dayr shnooller
during	während	vayrent
during the day	tagsüber	targsueber

E

ear	das Ohr	dass oa-er
ear, nose and throat (ENT)	der Hals-, Nasen-	dayr halz-, narzen-,
specialist	Ohrenarzt (HNO)	oarenartst (har enn oh)
earache	die Ohrenschmerzen	dee oarenshmairtsen
eardrops	die Ohrentropfen	dee oarentropfen
early	früh	frueh
earrings	die Ohrringe	dee oarringer
earth	die Erde	dee erder
earthenware	die Keramik	dee kayrarmik
east	der Osten	dayr osten
easy	leicht/(comfortable)	laikht/
	bequem	bekvaym
eat	essen	essen
eczema	das Ekzem	dass ektsaym
eel	der Aal	dayr arl
egg	das Ei	dass ai
elastic band	das Gummi	dass goomee
electric	elektrisch	elektrish
electricity	der Strom	dayr shtroam
embassy	die Botschaft	dee boatshaft
emergency brake	die Notbremse	dee noat bremzer
emergency exit	der Notausgang	dayr noat owsgang
emergency number	die Notrufnummer	dee noat roof noommer
emergency phone	die Notrufsäule	dee noat roof zoyler
emery board	die Nagelfeile	dee nargelfailer
empty	leer	layr
engaged (to be married)	verlobt	fayrloabt
engaged	besetzt	bezetst
England	England	englant
English	englisch	english
Englishman	der Engländer	dayr englender
Englishwoman	die Engländerin	dee englenderin
enjoy	genießen	geneessen
entertainment guide	der Veranstaltungs-	dayr fayr anshtal toongs
	kalender	kalender
envelope	der Umschlag	dayr umshlark
escort	die Begleitung	dee beglaitoong
evening	der Abend	dayr arbent
evening wear	die Abendkleidung	dee arbent klai doong
event	die Veranstaltung	dee fair an shtal toong
every time	jedesmal	yaydezmarl

everything	alles	*alless*
everywhere	überall	*ueberarl*
examine	untersuchen	*oonter zookhen*
excavation	die Ausgrabung	*dee owsgrarboong*
excellent	ausgezeichnet	*ows getsaikh net*
exchange	(aus)tauschen	*(ows)towshen*
exchange office	das Wechselbüro	*dass vekhsel buero*
exchange rate	der Wechselkurs	*dayr vekhselkoors*
excursion	der Ausflug	*dayr owsflook*
exhibition	die Ausstellung	*dee owsshteloong*
exit	der Ausgang	*dayr owsgang*
expenses	die Unkosten	*dee oonkosten*
expensive	teuer	*toyer*
explain	erklären	*ayrklayren*
express	der Schnellzug	*dayr shnelltsoog*
external	äusserlich	*oysserlikh*
eye	das Auge	*dass owger*
eyedrops	die Augentropfen	*dee owgentropfen*
eyeshadow	der Lidschatten	*dayr leetshatten*
eye specialist	der Augenarzt	*dayr owgenartst*
eyeliner	der Eyeliner	*dayr ailainer*

F

face	das Gesicht	*dass gezikht*
factory	die Fabrik	*dee fabreek*
fair	die Kirmes	*dee keermess*
fall	stürzen/fallen	*shtuertsen/fallen*
family	die Familie	*dee fameelier*
famous	berühmt	*beruemt*
far away	weit weg	*vait vek*
farm	der Bauernhof	*dayr bowernhoaf*
farmer	der Bauer	*dayr bower*
farmer's wife	die Bäuerin	*dee boyerin*
fashion	die Mode	*dee moader*
fast	schnell	*shnell*
father	der Vater	*dayr farter*
fault	die Schuld	*dee shoolt*
fax	telefaxen	*teleefaksen*
February	der Februar	*dayr febrooar*
	(Aus.) der Feber	*dayr fayber*
feel	fühlen	*fuelen*
feel like	Lust haben	*loost harben*
fence	der Zaun	*dayr tsown*
ferry	die Fähre	*dee fayrer*
fever	das Fieber	*dass feeber*
fill	füllen	*fuelen*
fill out	ausfüllen	*owsfuellen*
filling	die Füllung	*dee fuelloong*
film	der Film	*dayr film*
filter	der/das Filter	*dayr/dass filter*
find	finden	*finden*
fine	der Strafzettel	*dayr shtrarftsettel*
finger	der Finger	*dayr finger*
fire	das Feuer	*das foyer*
fire brigade	die Feuerwehr	*dee foyer vayr*
fire escape	die Feuertreppe	*dee foyer trepper*
fire extinguisher	der Feuerlöscher	*dayr foyer loesher*

first	erst/erste/erster	*ayrst/ayrster/ayrster*
first aid	die Erste Hilfe	*dee ayrster hilfer*
first class	erster Klasse	*ayrster klasser*
fish (verb)	angeln	*angeln*
fish	der Fisch	*dayr fish*
fishing rod	die Angel	*dee angel*
fit	passen	*passen*
fitness centre	das Fitness-Zentrum	*dass fitness-tsentroom*
fitness training	das Fitness-Training	*dass fitness-trayneeng*
fitting room	die Anprobekabine	*dee an prober kabeener*
fix	flicken	*flikken*
flag	die Fahne/die Flagge	*dee farner/dee flagger*
flash bulb	das Blitzbirnchen	*dass blitz birn khen*
flash cube	der Blitzwürfel	*dayr blitzvuerfel*
flash gun	das Blitzgerät	*dass blitzgerayt*
flat	die Etagenwohnung	*dee etarjen voh noong*
flea market	der Flohmarkt	*dayr flohmarkt*
flight	der Flug	*dayr flook*
flight number	die Flugnummer	*dee flooknoommer*
flood	die Überschwem- mung	*dee ueber shwem moong*
floor	der Stock/die Etage	*dayr shtok/dee etarjer*
flounder	die Flunder	*dee floonder*
flour	das Mehl	*dass mayhl*
flu	die Grippe	*dee gripper*
fly (insect)	die Fliege	*dee fleeger*
fly (verb)	fliegen	*fleegen*
fly-over	das Viadukt	*dass fiadookt*
fog	der Nebel	*dayr naybel*
foggy (to be)	neblig sein	*nayblikh zain*
folding caravan	der Faltwagen	*dayr faltvargen*
folkloristic	folkloristisch	*folkloristish*
follow	folgen	*folgen*
food	Lebensmittel	*laybens mittel*
food poisoning	die Lebensmittel- vergiftung	*dee laybenzmittel fairgif toong*
foot	der Fuss	*dayr fooss*
for	vor	*for*
forbidden	verboten	*fairboaten*
forehead	die Stirn	*dee shtirn*
foreign	ausländisch	*owslendish*
forget	vergessen	*fairgessen*
fork	die Gabel	*dee garbel*
form	das Formular	*dass formoolar*
fort	die Festung	*dee festoong*
forward	nachschicken	*nakhshikken*
fountain	der Springbrunnen	*dayr shpring broonnen*
frame	das Gestell	*dass geshtel*
franc	der Franken	*dayr franken*
free	frei	*frai*
free	gratis	*grartis*
free time	die Freizeit	*dee fraitsait*
freeze	gefrieren	*gefreeyeren*
French	französisch	*frantsoezish*
French bread	das Stangenweiss brot/die Baguette	*dass shtangenvaiss broat/dee baguetter*

fresh	frisch	*frish*
Friday	der Freitag	*dayr fraitark*
fried	gebacken	*gebacken*
fried egg	das Spiegelei	*dass shpeegelai*
friend	der Freund	*dayr froynt*
friendly	freundlich	*froyntlikh*
frightened	ängstlich	*enkstlikh*
fruit	das Obst	*dass oapst*
fruit juice	der Obstsaft	*dayr oapstzaft*
frying pan	die (Brat)pfanne	*dee (brart)pfanner*
full	voll	*foll*
fun	das Vergnügen/	*dass fergnuegen/*
	der Spass	*dayr shpass*

G

gallery	die Galerie	*dee galleree-er*
game	das Spiel(chen)	*dass shpeel(khen)*
garage	die Werkstatt	*dee verkshtatt*
garbage bag	der Müllsack	*dayr muelzak*
garden	der Garten	*dayr garten*
gas (propane camping)	das Campinggas	*dass kamping gas*
	(das Propangas)	*(dass proaparn gas)*
gastroenteritis	die Magen- und	*dee margen- oont*
	Darmbeschwerden	*darmbeshvayrden*
gate	das Tor	*dass torr*
gauze	der Verbandmull	*dayr fayrbantmool*
gear	der Gang	*dayr gang*
gel	das Gel	*dass jel*
German	deutsch	*doytsh*
Germany	Deutschland	*doytshlant*
get lost	sich verirren	*zikh fayreeren*
get married	heiraten	*hai-rarten*
get off	aussteigen	*owsshtaigen*
gift	das Geschenk	*dass geshenk*
gilt	vergoldet	*fairgoldet*
ginger	der Ingwer	*dayr ingver*
girl	das Mädchen	*dass maydkhen*
girlfriend	die Freundin	*dee froyndin*
giro cheque	der Postbarscheck	*dayr posst barshek*
giro pass	die Giroscheckkarte	*dee geero shek karter*
glacier	der Gletscher	*dayr gletsher*
glass	das Glas	*dass glas*
glasses (sun)	die Sonnenbrille	*dee zonnen briller*
gliding	das Segelfliegen	*dass zaygel fleegen*
glove	der Handschuh	*dayr hantshoo*
glue	der Klebstoff	*dayr klaypshtoff*
gnat	die Mücke	*dee muekker*
go (on foot)	gehen	*gayhen*
go back	zurückgehen/(car)	*tsueruek gayhen/*
	zurückfahren	*tsueruek faren*
go out	ausgehen	*owsgayhen*
goat's cheese	der Ziegenkäse	*dayr tseegen kayzer*
gold	das Gold	*dass golt*
golf	das Golfspiel	*dass golfshpeel*
golf course	der Golfplatz	*dayr golfplats*
gone	weg	*vek*

good day	guten Tag	gooten tark
	(Aus. servus)	zairvoos
	(Sw. Grüezi)	gruetsee
good evening	guten Abend	gooten arbent
good morning	guten Morgen	gooten morgen
good night	gute Nacht	gooter nakht
goodbye	der Abschied	dayr apsheet
gram	das Gramm	dass gramm
grandchild	das Enkelkind	dass enkelkint
grandfather	der Opa	dayr oapa
grandmother	die Oma	dee oamar
grape juice	der Traubensaft	dayr trowbenzaft
grapefruit	die Pampelmuse	dee pampel moozer
grapes	die (Wein)trauben	dee (vain)trowben
grave	das Grab	dass grarp
grease	das Fett	dass fett
green	grün	gruen
green card	die grüne Karte	dee gruener karter
greet	begrüssen	begruessen
grey	grau	grow
grill	grillen	grillen
grilled	geröstet	geroestet
grocer	der Kaufmann/	dayr kowfmann/
	Gemüsehändler	gemueser haentler
ground	der Boden	dayr boaden
group	die Gruppe	dee grupper
guest house	die Pension	dee penseeoan
guide (person/book)	der Führer	dayr fuehrer
guided tour	die Führung	dee fueroong
gynaecologist	der Frauenarzt	dayr frowenartst

H

hair	das Haar	dass har
hairbrush	die Haarbürste	dee harbuerster
hairdresser	der Damen-, Herren-	dayr darmen-, hayrren
	frisör	frizoer
hairpins	die Haarnadeln/	dee harnardeln/
	Haarklemmen	harklemmen
hairspray	das Haarspray	dass harspray
half	halb	halp
half	die Hälfte	dee helfter
half full	halb voll	halp foll
ham (boiled)	der Kochschinken	dayr kokhshinken
ham (smoked)	der Räucherschinken	dayr roykher shinken
hammer	der Hammer	dayr hammer
hand	die Hand	dee hant
handbrake	die Handbremse	dee hantbremzer
handbag	die Handtasche	dee hant-tasher
handkerchief	das Taschentuch	dass tashentookh
handmade	handgearbeitet	hant ge ar bai tet
happy	froh	fro
harbour	der Hafen	dayr harfen
hard	hart	hart
hat	der Hut	dayr hoot
hat	die Mütze	dee muetser
hayfever	der Heuschnupfen	dayr hoyshnoopfen
hazelnut	die Haselnuss	dee harzelnooss

Word list

head	der Kopf	*dayr kopf*
headache	die Kopfschmerzen	*dee kopf shmer tsen*
health	die Gesundheit	*dee gezoonthait*
health food shop	das Reformgeschäft	*dass reform gesheft*
hear	hören	*hoeren*
hearing aid	das Hörgerät	*dass hoergerayt*
heart	das Herz	*dass hayrts*
heart patient	der Herzkranke	*dayr hayrts kranker*
heater	die Heizung	*dee haitsoong*
heavy	schwer	*shvayr*
heel	die Ferse	*dee fayrzer*
heel (shoe)	der Absatz	*dayr apzats*
hello	Hallo	*hullo*
helmet	der Helm	*dayr helm*
help	helfen	*helfen*
help	die Hilfe	*dee hilfer*
helping	die Portion	*dee portseeyoan*
herbal tea	der Kräutertee	*dayr kroytertay*
herbs	die Gewürze/(green)	*dee gevuertser/*
	die Kräuter	*dee kroyter*
here	hier	*heer*
here you are	(giving sb sth) hier/	*heer/dar bist doo yar/*
	(on finding sb) da	*dar ist ez yar*
	bist du ja!/(on finding	
	sth) da ist es ja!	
herring	der Hering	*dayr hayring*
high	hoch	*hokh*
high tide	die Flut	*dee floot*
highchair	der Kinderstuhl	*dayr kindershtool*
hiking	der Wandersport	*dayr vandershport*
hiking trip	die Wanderung	*dee vanderoong*
hip	die Hüfte	*dee huefter*
hire (for)	zu vermieten	*tsoo fairmeeten*
hire	mieten	*meeten*
hitchhike	per Anhalter fahren/	*payr anhalter faren/*
	trampen	*trampen*
hobby	das Hobby	*dass hobby*
holiday	der Feiertag	*dayr fayertark*
holiday	die Ferien/der Urlaub	*dee fayreeyen/dayr*
		oorlowp
holiday house	die Ferienwohnung	*dee fayreeyen voanoong*
holiday park	der Bungalowpark	*der bungaloapark*
homesickness	das Heimweh	*dass haimvay*
honest	ehrlich	*ayrlikh*
honey	der Honig	*dayr hoanikh*
horizontal	horizontal	*horeetsontarl*
horrible	scheusslich	*shoyslikh*
horse	das Pferd	*dass pfayrt*
hospital	das Krankenhaus	*dass krankenhowz*
	(Aus.,Sw.) das	*dass hospitarl*
	Hospital/Spital	*dass shpitarl*
hospitality	die Gastfreundschaft	*dee gast froynt shaft*
hot (spicy)	pikant	*peekant*
hot-water bottle	die Wärmflasche	*dee vayrm flasher*
hotel	das Hotel	*dass hotel*
hour	die Stunde	*dee shtoonder*
house	das Haus	*dass howz*

household items	die Haushaltsartikel	dee howz halts artee kel
Houses of Parliament	das Parlaments- gebäude	dass parlaments geboyder
housewife	die Hausfrau	dee hows frow
how far?	wie weit?	vee vait?
how long?	wie lange?	vee langer?
how much?	wieviel?	veefeel?
how?	wie?	vee?
hungry (to be)	hungrig	hoongrikh
hurricane	der Orkan	dayr orkarn
hurry	die Eile	dee ailer
husband	der (Ehe) mann	dayr (ayher) man
hut (mountain)	die Berghütte	dee bairghuetter
hut	die Hütte	dee huetter
hyperventilation	die Hyperventilation	dee hueper ventee la tseeoan

I

ice cubes	die Eiswürfel	dee aiz vuer fell
ice skating	das Schlittschuh- laufen	dass shlit shoo lowfen
icecream	das (Speise)eis	dass shpaizeraiz
idea	die Idee	dee eeday
identification	der Ausweis	dayr owsvaiss
identify	identifizieren	eedentee fi tsee ren
ill	krank	krank
illness	die Krankheit	dee krankhait
imagination	die Vorstellung	dee forshtelloong
immediately	sofort	zofort
import duty	Einfuhrzölle	ainfoor tsoeller
impossible	unmöglich	oonmoeglikh
in	in	in
in the evening	abends	arbents
in the morning	morgens	morgens
included	enthalten/ einschliesslich	enthalten/ ainshleesslikh
indicate	zeigen	tsaigen
indicator	der Blinker	dayr blinker
industrial art	das Kunstgewerbe	dass koonstgewayrber
inexpensive	billig	billikh
infection (viral, bacterial)	die Virusinfektion, die bakterielle Infektion	dee veeroos infekts eeoan, dee bakteereey eller infektseeoan
inflammation	die Entzündung	dee ent tsuen doong
information	die Angaben	dee angarben
information	die Auskunft	dee owskunft
information office	das Auskunftsbüro	dass ows kunfts bueroh
injection	die Spritze	dee shpritser
injured	verletzt	fayrletst
innocent	unschuldig	oonshooldikh
insect	das Insekt	dass inzekt
insect bite	der Insektenstich	dayr inzekten shtikh
insect repellent	das Mückenöl	dass muekkenoel
inside	drin(nen)	drin(nen)
insole	die Einlegesohle	dee ainlaygesohler

Word list

instructions	die Gebrauchs-anweisung	*dee gebrowkhs anvai zoong*
insurance	die Versicherung	*dee fayrzikheroong*
intermission	die Pause	*dee powzer*
international	international	*eenter natseeoa narl*
interpreter	der Dolmetscher	*dayr dolmetsher*
intersection	die Kreuzung	*dee kroytsoong*
introduce oneself	sich vorstellen	*sikh forshtellen*
invite	einladen	*ainlarden*
iodine	das Jod	*dass yot*
Ireland	Irland	*eerlant*
Irish	irländisch	*eerlendish*
Irishman	der Ire	*dayr eerer*
Irishwoman	die Irin	*dee eerin*
iron (verb)	bügeln	*byoogelln*
iron	das Bügeleisen	*dass buegell aizen*
ironing board	das Bügelbrett	*dass buegelbrett*
island	die Insel	*dee inzel*
Italian	italienisch	*italeeaynish*
Italy	Italien	*itarlee-en*
itch	das Jucken	*dass yooken*

J

jack	der Wagenheber	*dayr vargen hayber*
jacket	die Jacke	*dee yakker*
jam	die Marmelade	*dee marmelarder*
January	der Januar (Aus.) der Jenner	*dayr yanooar/ dayr yenner*
jaw	der Kiefer	*dayr keefer*
jellyfish	die Qualle	*dee kvaller*
jeweller	der Juwelier	*dayr yoovayleer*
jewellery	der Schmuck	*dayr shmook*
jog	joggen	*joggen*
joke	der Witz	*dayr vits*
juice	der Saft	*dayr zaft*
July	der Juli	*dayr yoolee*
jumble sale	der Flohmarkt	*dayr flohmarkt*
jump leads	das Startkabel	*dass shtartkarbel*
jumper	der Pullover	*dayr pullover*
June	der Juni	*dayr yooni*

K

key (ignition)	der Zündschlüssel	*dayr tsuent shluessel*
key	der Schlüssel	*dayr shluessel*
kilo	das Kilo	*dass keelo*
kilometre	der Kilometer	*dayr keelo mayter*
king	der König	*dayr koenikh*
kiss (verb)	küssen	*kuessen*
kiss	der Kuss	*dayr kooss*
kitchen	die Küche	*dee kuekher*
knee	das Knie	*dass knee*
knee socks	Kniestrümpfe	*dee knee shtruempfer*
knife	das Messer	*dass messer*
knit	stricken	*shtrikken*
know	wissen	*vissen*

L

lace	der Schnürsenkel	*dayr shnuerzenkel*
ladies toilet	die Damentoilette	*dee darmen twalet ter*
lake	der See	*dayr zay*
lamp	die Lampe	*dee lamper*
land	landen	*landen*
lane	die Fahrspur	*dee fahrshpoor*
language	die Sprache	*dee shprakher*
large	gross	*groass*
last	letzte	*letster*
late	spät	*shpayt*
later	nachher	*nakh her*
laugh	lachen	*lakhen*
launderette	die Münzwäscherei	*dee muents vesheray*
law	das Recht	*dass rekht*
laxative	das Abführmittel	*dass ap fuer mittel*
leaded	das Super(benzin)	*dass zooper(bentseen)*
leak	das Loch	*dass lokh*
leather	das Leder	*dass layder*
leather goods	Lederwaren	*layder varen*
leave	abfahren/abfliegen	*apfahren/apfleegen*
leek	der Porree/der Lauch	*dayr porray/dayr lowkh*
left	links	*links*
left	nach links	*nakh links*
leg	das Bein	*dass bain*
lemon	die Zitrone	*dee tsitroner*
lend	leihen	*laihen*
lens (wide-angle)	das Weitwinkel-objektiv	*dass vait vinkel obyek teef*
lens	die Linse	*dee linzer*
lentils	die Linsen	*dee linzen*
less	weniger	*vayniger*
lesson	die Stunde	*dee shtoonder*
letter	der Brief	*dayr breef*
lettuce	der Kopfsalat	*dayr kopfzalart*
level crossing	der Bahnübergang	*dayr barn ueber gang*
library	die Bibliothek	*dee beebleeotayk*
lie (tell lie)	lügen	*luegen*
lie	liegen	*leegen*
lift (hitchhike)	die Mitfahr-gelegenheit	*dee mit far-gelaygenhait*
lift (in building)	der Fahrstuhl/der Aufzug	*dayr farshtool/ der owftsook*
lift (ski)	der (Sessel)lift	*dayr (zessel)lift*
light (not dark)	hell	*hell*
light (not heavy)	leicht	*laikht*
lighter	das Feuerzeug	*dass foyer tsoyk*
lighthouse	der Leuchtturm	*dayr loykht toorm*
lightning	der Blitz	*dayr blits*
like	mögen/(stronger) lieben	*moergen/leeben*
line	die Linie	*dee leenier*
linen	das Leinen	*dass lainen*
lipstick	der Lippenstift	*dayr lippen shtift*
liqueur	der Likör	*dayr leekoer*
liquorice	die Lakritze(n)	*dee lakritzer(n)*
listen	(zu)hören	*(tsoo)hoeren*

Word list

literature	die Literatur	*dee literatoor*
litre	der/das Liter	*dayr/dass leeter*
little	wenig	*vaynikh*
little (a)	das bisschen, ein bisschen	*dass bis-shen, ain bis-shen*
live	wohnen	*voanen*
live together	zusammenleben	*tsoo zammen layben*
lobster	der Hummer	*dayr hoommer*
local	örtlich	*oertlikh*
lock	das Schloss	*dass shloss*
locker (luggage)	das Schliessfach (für Gepäck)	*dass shleesfakh (fuer gepek)*
long	lang	*lang*
look	schauen	*showern*
look for	suchen	*zookhen*
look up	aufsuchen	*owfzookhen*
lorry	der LKW/der Lastwagen	*dayr ellkarvay/dayr lasstvargen*
lose	verlieren	*fayrleeren*
loss	der Verlust	*dayr fayrloost*
lost	(gen.)weg/(also people) vermisst	*vek/fayrmisst*
lost	verloren	*fayrloren*
lost property office	das Fundbüro	*dass foontbuero*
lotion	die Lotion	*dee loatseeoan*
loud	laut	*lowt*
love	sich lieben	*zikh leeben*
love	die Liebe	*dee leeber*
low	niedrig	*needrikh*
low tide	die Ebbe	*dee ebber*
luck	das Glück	*dass gluek*
luggage (left)	die Gepäckaufbewahrung	*dee gepek owfbevaroong*
luggage	das Gepäck	*dass gepek*
luggage locker	das Schliessfach	*dass shleesfakh*
lumps (sugar)	die Zuckerwürfel	*dee tsooker wuerfel*
lunch	das Mittagessen	*dass mittark essen*
lungs	die Lungen	*dee loongen*

M

macaroni	Makkaroni	*makaroanee*
machine (vending)	der Automat	*dayr owtomart*
madam	meine Dame	*mainer darmer*
magazine	die Zeitschrift	*dee tsaitshrift*
mail	die Post	*dee post*
make an appointment	einen Termin machen	*ainen tairmeen makhen*
makeshift	provisorisch	*proveezorish*
manager	der Verwalter	*dayr fayrvalter*
mandarin	die Mandarine	*dee mandareener*
manicure	die Maniküre	*dee manee kuerer*
map	die (Land)karte	*dee (lant)karter*
marble	der Marmor	*dayr marmor*
March	der März	*dayr mayrts*
margarine	die Margarine	*dee margareener*
marina	der Yachthafen	*dayr yakht harfen*
market	der Markt	*dayr markt*

Word list

marriage	die Ehe	*dee ayher*
married	verheiratet	*fayrhai-rartet*
mass	die Messe	*dee messer*
massage	die Massage	*dee massarjer*
match	der Wettkampf	*dayr vetkampf*
matches	die Streichhölzer	*dee shtraikh hoeltser*
May	der Mai	*dayr mai*
maybe	vielleicht	*feelaikht*
mayonnaise	die Mayonnaise	*dee mayonnayzer*
mayor	der Bürgermeister	*dayr buerger maister*
meal	die Mahlzeit	*dee marltsait*
mean	bedeuten	*bedoyten*
meat	das Fleisch	*dass flaish*
medication	das Heilmittel	*dass hailmittel*
medicine	das Medikament	*dass medee kar ment*
meet	kennenlernen	*kennen layrnen*
melon	die Melone	*dee melowner*
membership	die Mitgliedschaft	*dee mitt gleet shaft*
menstruate	(meine/ihre) Tage haben	*(mainer/eerer) targer harben*
menstruation	die Periode	*dee peereeoader*
menu	das Menü	*dass menue*
menu	die Speisekarte	*dee shpaizer karter*
menu of the day	das Tagesmenü	*dass targez menue*
message	der Bescheid/die Nachricht	*dayr beshait/dee nakhrikht*
metal	das Metall	*dass mettarl*
meter	der/das Taxameter	*dayr/dass taksamayter*
metre	der/das Meter	*dayr/dass mayter*
migraine	die Migräne	*dee meegrayner*
mild (tobacco)	(der) leicht(e) (Tabak)	*(dayr) laikht(er) (tarbak)*
milk	die Milch	*dee milkh*
millimetre	der/das Millimeter	*dayr/dass millimayter*
milometer	der Kilometerzähler	*dayr keelo mayter tsayler*
mince	das Mett/das Hackfleisch	*dass met/dass hackflaish*
mineral water	das Mineralwasser	*dass minerarl vasser*
minute	die Minute	*dee meenooter*
mirror	der Spiegel	*dayr shpeegell*
miss	vermissen	*fayrmissen*
missing (to be)	fehlen	*faylen*
missing person	vermisste Person	*fayrmisster payrzoan*
mistake	der Fehler/der Irrtum	*dayr fayler/dayr eertoom*
mistaken (to be)	sich irren	*zikh irren*
misunderstanding	das Missverständnis	*dass miss fayr shtant nis*
mocha	der Mokka	*dayr mokker*
modern art	die moderne Kunst	*dee moderner koonst*
molar	der Backenzahn	*dayr bakkentsarn*
moment	der Augenblick	*dayr owgenblik*
moment	der Moment	*dayr moament*
monastery	das Kloster	*dass kloaster*
Monday	der Montag	*dayr moantark*
money	das Geld	*dass gelt*
month	der Monat	*dayr moanart*
moped	das Moped	*dass moaped*
mosque	die Moschee	*dee moshay*

135

motel	das Motel	dass moatell
mother	die Mutter	dee mooter
moto-cross	das Moto-Cross	dass moto-kross
motorbike	das Motorrad	dass moatorrart
motorboat	das Motorboot	dass moatorboot
motorway	die Autobahn	dee owtobarn
mountain	der Berg	dayr bayrk
mountaineering	der Bergsport	dayr bayrk shporrt
mouse	die Maus	dee mows
mouth	der Mund	dayr munt
much/many	viel	feel
muscle	der Muskel	dayr mooskel
muscle spasms	die Muskelkrämpfe	dee mooskel krempfer
museum	das Museum	dass moozayoom
mushrooms	die Pilze	dee piltser
music	die Musik	dee moozeek
musical	das Musical	dass moozeekall
mussels	die Muscheln	dee moosheln
mustard	der Senf/der Mostrich	dayr zenf/dayr mosstrikh

N

nail	der Nagel	dayr nargel
nail polish	der Nagellack	dayr nargellack
nail polish remover	der Nagellack-entferner	nargel lack entfair ner
nail scissors	die Nagelschere	dee nargelsheerer
naked	nackt	nakt
nappy	die Windel	dee vindel
National Health Service	die Krankenkasse	dee kranken kasser
nationality	die Staatsangehörig-keit	dee shtarts an gehoerig kait
natural	natürlich	natuerlikh
nature	die Natur	dee natoor
naturism	die Freikörperkultur	dee fray koerper kooltoor
nauseous	übel	uebel
near	bei	bai
nearby	in der Nähe	in dayr nayher
necessary	nötig/notwendig	noetikh/noatvendikh
neck	der Nacken	dayr nakken
necklace	die Kette	dee ketter
nectarine	die Nektarine	dee nektareener
needle	die Nadel	dee nardel
negative	das Negativ	dass negateef
neighbours	die Nachbarn	dee nakhbarn
nephew	der Neffe	dayr neffer
never	nie	nee
new	neu	noy
news	die Nachricht	dee nakhrikht
news-stand	der Kiosk	dayr keeosk
newspaper	die Zeitung	dee tsaitoong
next	nächste(r)	nekhste(r)
next to	neben	nayben
nice (friendly)/nice (to the eye)	nett/hübsch	nett/huepsh
nice (cosy)	gemütlich	gemuetlikh

nice (delicious)	lecker	*lekker*
niece	die Nichte	*dee nikhter*
night	die Nacht	*dee nakht*
night (at)	nachts	*nakhts*
night duty	der Nachtdienst	*dayr nakhtdeenst*
nightclub	der Nachtklub	*dayr nakhtkloop*
nightlife	das Nachtleben	*dass nakhtlayben*
no	nein	*nain*
no overtaking	das Überholverbot	*dass ueber hoal fayr boat*
noise	der Lärm	*dayr layrm*
nonstop	nonstop	*nonstop*
no-one	niemand/keiner	*neemant/kainer*
normal	gewöhnlich	*gevoehnlikh*
north	der Norden	*der norden*
normal	normal	*normarl*
north	nördlich	*noerdlikh*
nose	die Nase	*dee narzer*
nose drops	Nasentropfen	*narzen tropfen*
nosebleed	das Nasenbluten	*dass narzen blooten*
notepaper	das Briefpapier	*dass breefpapeer*
nothing	nichts	*nikhts*
November	der November	*dayr november*
nowhere	nirgendwo	*neergentvo*
nude beach	der Nackt(bade)strand	*dayr nakt(barderr) shtrant*
number	die Nummer	*dee noommer*
number (subscriber's)	die Rufnummer	*dee roof noommer*
number plate	das Nummernschild	*dass noommern shilt*
nurse	die (Kranken)-schwester	*dee (kranken)shvester*
nutmeg	die Muskatnuss	*dee mooskartnooss*
nuts	die Nüsse	*dee nuesser*

O

October	der Oktober	*dayr oktoaber*
off (food)	verdorben	*fairdorben*
offer	anbieten	*anbeeten*
office	das Büro	*dass buero*
off-licence	der Spirituosen-händler	*dayr shpiri too oazen hendler*
oil (diesel)	das Dieselöl	*dass deezeloel*
oil	das Öl	*dass oel*
oil change	der Ölwechsel	*dayr oelvekhsel*
oil level	der Ölstand	*dayr oelshtant*
ointment	die Salbe	*dee zalber*
okay	einverstanden	*ain fayr shtanden*
old	alt	*alt*
olive oil	das Olivenöl	*dass oleevenoel*
olives	die Oliven	*dee oleeven*
omelette	das Omelett	*dass ommlett*
on	auf	*owf*
on the right	rechts	*rekhts*
on the way	unterwegs	*oontervaygs*
oncoming traffic	der Gegenverkehr	*dayr gaygen fayrkayr*
one hundred grams	hundert Gramm	*hoondert gramm*
one-way-traffic	der Einbahnverkehr	*dayr ain barn fayrkayr*
onion	die Zwiebel	*dee tsveebel*

Word list

open	öffnen	*oeffnen*
open	offen	*offen*
opera	die Oper	*dee oaper*
operate	operieren	*opereeren*
operator (telephone)	(m) der Telefonist/(f) die Telefonistin	*der telefoanist/ dee telefoanistin*
operetta	die Operette	*dee operetter*
opposite	gegenüber	*gaygenueber*
optician	der Optiker	*dayr optiker*
or	oder	*oader*
orange	die Apfelsine/die Orange	*dee apfel zeener/ dee oranje*
orange juice	der Orangensaft	*dayr oranjenzaft*
order	die Bestellung	*dee beshtelloong*
order (in), tidy	in Ordnung	*in ordnoong*
order	bestellen	*beshtellen*
other	andere/-s	*anderer/-s*
other side	die andere Seite	*dee anderer zaiter*
outside	(dr)aussen/(out wards) raus	*(dr)owssen, rows*
overtake	(overtake) überholen/ (come alongside) einholen	*ueber hoalen/ ainhoalen*
oysters	die Austern	*dee owstern*

P

packed lunch	das Lunchpaket	*dass loonch pakayt*
pad (writing)	der Schreibblock (squared, lined)	*dayr shraipblok*
page	die Seite	*dee zaiter*
pain	der Schmerz, (pl.) Schmerzen	*dayr shmayrts, shmayrtsen*
painkiller	das Schmerzmittel	*dass shmayrts mittel*
paint	die Farbe	*dee farber*
painting (art)	die Malerei	*dee marlerai*
painting (object)	das Gemälde	*dass gemelder*
palace	der Palast	*dayr palast*
pan	derTopf	*dayr topf*
pancake	der Eierkuchen/ der Pfannkuchen	*dayr aierkookhen/ dayr pfann kookhen*
pane	die Scheibe	*dee shayber*
panties	der Slip	*dayr slip*
pants	die Unterhose(n)	*dee oonterhoaze(n)*
panty liner	die Slipeinlage	*dee shlip ain larger*
paper	das Papier	*dass papeer*
paper (writing)	das Schreibpapier	*dass shraip papeer*
paprika	der Paprika	*dayr papreeker*
paraffin oil	das Petroleum	*dass petrolayoom*
parasol	der Sonnenschirm	*dayr zonnensheerm*
parcel	das Paket/das Päckchen	*dass pakayt/dass pekshen*
pardon	die Entschuldigung/ die Verzeihung	*dee entshool dee goong/dee fayrtsayoong*
parents	die Eltern	*dee elltern*

park	der Park	dayr park
park (car)	parken/ (Sw.) parkieren	parken/ parkeeren
parking space	der Parkplatz	dayr parkplats
parsley	die Petersilie	dee payterzeelier
part	das (Ersatz)teil	dass (ayrzats)tail
partition	die Trennwand	dee trennwant
partner	der Partner	dayr partner
party	das Fest/die Party	dass fest/dee party
passable	begehbar/(vehicle) befahrbar	begaybar, befarbar
passenger	der Passagier	dayr passajeer
passport	der (Reise)pass	dayr (raizer)parss
passport photo	das Passbild	dass passbilt
patient	der Patient	dayr patseeyent
pavement	der Gehsteig/ das Trottoir	dayr gayshtaik/ dass trottwar
pay	(be)zahlen	(be)tsarlen
pay the bill	abrechnen	aprekhnen
peach	der Pfirsich	dayr pfeerzikh
peanuts	die Erdnüsse	dee ertnuesser
pear	die Birne	dee beerner
peas	die Erbsen	dee airpsen
pedal	das Pedal	dass pedarl
pedicure	die Fusspflege	dee fusspflayger
pen	der Stift	dayr shtift
pencil	der Bleistift	dayr blaishtift
penis	der Penis	dayr payniss
pension	die Pension	dee ponseeyoan
pepper	der Pfeffer	dayr pfeffer
performance	die Theatervorstel- lung	dee tayartter for shtelloong
perfume	das Parfüm	dass parfuem
perm (to have a)	eine Dauerwelle machen	einer dowerveller makhen
perm	die Dauerwelle	dee dowerveller
permit	die Genehmigung/ die Erlaubnis	dee genay migoong/ dee erlowpniss
person	die Person	dee payrzoan
personal	persönlich	payrzoenlikh
petrol	das Benzin	dass bentseen
petrol station	die Tankstelle	dee tank shteller
pets	die Haustiere	dee howz teerer
pharmacy	die Apotheke	dee appotayker
phone (tele-)	das Telefon	dass talayfoan
phone	telefonieren	taylayfoaneeren
phone box	die Telefonzelle	dee taylayfoan tseller
phone directory	das Telefonbuch	dass taylayfoan bookh
phone number	die Telefonnummer	dee taylayfown noomer
photo	das Foto	dass foto
photocopier	das Kopiergerät	dass kopee gerayt
photocopy	fotokopieren	foto kopeeren
photocopy	die Fotokopie	dee fotokopee
pick up (an object)	aufheben	owfhayben
pick up	(ab)holen	(ap)hoalen
picnic	das Picknick	dass piknik

Word list

pier	die Landungsbrücke	*dee landoongz brueker*
pigeon	die Taube	*dee towber*
pill (contraceptive)	die Pille	*dee piller*
pill (morning-after)	die Pille danach	*dee piller danakh*
pillow	das Kissen	*dass kissen*
pillowcase	der Kissenüberzug	*dayr kissen ueber tsook*
pin	die Stecknadel	*dee shteknardel*
pineapple	die Ananas	*dee anarnass*
pipe	die Pfeife	*dee pfaifer*
pipe tobacco	der Pfeifentabak	*dayr pfaifen tarbak*
pity	schade	*sharder*
place of interest	die Sehenswürdigkeit	*dee zayenz vuerdeekh kait*
plan	der Plan	*dayr plarn*
plant	die Pflanze	*dee pflantser*
plasters	das (Heft)pflaster	*dass (heft)pflaster*
plastic	das Plastik	*dass plastik*
plastic bag	die Tüte	*dee tueter*
plate	der Teller	*dayr teller*
platform	das Gleis	*dass glais*
platform	der Bahnsteig	*dayr barnshtaik*
play (theatre)	das Theaterstück	*dass tayarter shtuek*
play	spielen	*shpeelen*
playground	der Spielplatz	*dayr shpeelplats*
playing cards	die Spielkarten	*dee shpeelkarten*
pleasant	angenehm	*angenaym*
please	bitte	*bitter*
pleasure	das Vergnügen	*dass fairgnuegen*
plum	die Pflaume	*dee pflowmer*
pocketknife	das Taschenmesser	*dass tashen messer*
point	zeigen	*tsaigen*
poison	das Gift	*dass gift*
police	die Polizei	*dee poleetsai*
police station	die Polizeiwache	*dee poleetsai vakher*
policeman	der Polizist	*dayr poleetsist*
pond	der Teich	*dayr taikh*
pony	das Pony	*dass poanee*
pop concert	das Popkonzert	*dass pop kontsert*
population	die Bevölkerung	*dee befoelke roong*
pork	das Schweinefleisch	*dass shvainerflaish*
port	der Port(wein)	*dayr port(vain)*
porter	der Pförtner	*dayr pfoertner*
porter	der Gepäckträger	*dayr gepek trayger*
post code	die Postleitzahl	*dee post lait tsarl*
post office	das Postamt	*dass postamt*
post office (main)	die Hauptpost	*dee howptpost*
postage	das Porto	*dass porto*
postbox	der Briefkasten	*dayr breef kasten*
postcard	die Ansichtskarte/die Postkarte	*dee ansikhts karter/ dee post karter*
postman	der Briefträger	*dayr breeftrayger*
potato	die Kartoffel	*dee kartoffell*
	(Aus.) die Heurigen	*dee hoyrigen*
poultry	das Geflügel	*dass gefluegel*

pound	das Pfund	*dass pfoont*
powdered milk	das Milchpulver	*dass milkhpulver*
power point	der Elektroanschluss	*dayr elektro anshluss*
pram	der Kinderwagen	*dayr kinder vargen*
prawns	die Garnelen	*dee garnaylen*
precious	lieb/teuer	*leep/toyer*
prefer	vorziehen	*fortseehen*
preference	die Vorliebe	*dee forleeber*
pregnant	schwanger/in anderen Umständen	*shvanger/in anderen oomshtenden*
present	vorhanden/(person) anwesend	*forhanden/ anvayzent*
present	das Geschenk	*dass geshenk*
press	drücken	*druekken*
pressure	der Druck	*dayr drook*
price	der Preis	*dayr praiss*
price list	die Preisliste	*dee praisslister*
print	abziehen	*aptseehen*
print	der Abzug	*dayr aptsook*
probably	wahrscheinlich	*varshainlikh*
problem	das Problem	*dass problaym*
profession	der Beruf	*dayr beroof*
programme	das Programm	*dass programm*
pronounce	aussprechen	*owsshprekhen*
pub	die Kneipe	*dee knaiper*
pudding	der Pudding	*dayr pudding*
pull	ziehen	*tseehen*
pull a muscle	sich einen Muskel verzerren	*zikh ainen mooskel fayrtserren*
pure	pur	*poor*
purple	lila	*leelar*
purse	der Geldbeutel	*dayr geltboytel*
purse	das Portemonnaie/die Börse	*dass portmonnay/dee boerzer*
push	schieben/drücken	*sheeben/drueken*
puzzle	das Puzzle	*dass puzzle (pootsel)*
pyjamas	der Pyjama	*dayr peejarmar*

Q

quarter	das Viertel	*dass feartell*
quarter of an hour	die Viertelstunde	*dee fear tell shtoonder*
queen	die Königin	*dee koenigin*
question	die Frage	*dee frager*
quick	schnell	*shnell*
quiet	ruhig	*roohikh*

R

radio	das Radio	*dass rardio*
railway	die (Bundes)bahn	*dee (boondez)barn*
rain	der Regen	*dayr raygen*
rain (verb)	regnen	*raygnen*
raincoat	der Regenmantel	*dayr raygenmantel*
raisins	die Rosinen	*dee rozeenen*
rape	die Vergewaltigung	*dee fair gevalti goong*
rapids	die Stromschnelle(n)	*dee shtroamshneller(n)*

rash	der Ausschlag	*dayr owsshlark*
raspberries	die Himbeeren	*dee himbeeren*
raw	roh	*roa*
raw vegetables	die Rohkost	*dee roakost*
razor blades	die Rasierklingen	*dee razeer klingen*
read	lesen	*layzen*
ready	fertig	*fairtikh*
really	eigentlich	*aigentlikh*
receipt (written)	der Empfangsschein	*dayr empfangs shain*
receipt (till-chit)	der Kassenzettel/die Quittung	*dayr kassentsettel/dee kvittoong*
recipe	das Rezept	*dass retsept*
reclining chair	der Liegestuhl	*dayr leegershtool*
recommend	empfehlen	*empfaylen*
recovery service	die Pannenhilfe	*dee pannen hilfer*
rectangle	das Rechteck	*dass rekhtekk*
red	rot	*roat*
red wine	der Rotwein	*dayr roatvain*
reduction	die Ermässigung	*dee ermayssigoong*
refrigerator	der Kühlschrank	*dayr kuelshrank*
region	die Gegend	*dee gaygent*
registration	der Kraftfahrzeug- schein	*dayr kraft far tsoyk shain*
relatives	die Verwandten	*dee fayrvanten*
reliable	zuverlässig	*tsoofayrlessikh*
religion	der Glaube(n)/die Religion	*dayr glowber(n)/die religioan*
rent out	vermieten	*fayrmeeten*
repair	reparieren	*repareeren*
repairs	die Reparatur	*dee reparatoor*
repeat	wiederholen	*veederhoalen*
report	die Anzeige	*dee antsaiger*
resent	übelnehmen	*uebel naymen*
reset	zurücksetzen	*tsooruek zetsen*
responsible	verantwortlich	*fayr antvort likh*
rest	ausruhen	*owsroohen*
restaurant	das Restaurant	*dass restorant*
result	das Ergebnis	*dass ergaypniss*
retired	pensioniert	*penzeeo neert*
return (ticket)	die Rückfahrkarte	*dee rueck far karter*
reverse (vehicle)	rückwärts fahren	*ruekverts faren*
rheumatism	das Rheuma	*dass roymar*
rice	der Reis	*dayr raiss*
ridiculous	unsinnig	*oonzinnikh*
riding (horseback)	das Reiten	*dass raiten*
riding school	die Reitschule	*dee raitshooler*
right	rechts	*rekhts*
right of way	die Vorfahrt	*dee forfart*
ripe	reif	*raif*
risk	das Risiko	*dass reezeeko*
river	der Fluss	*dayr flooss*
road	der Weg	*dayr vayk*
roadway	die Fahrbahn	*dee farbarn*
roasted	gebraten	*gebraten*
rock	der Fels(en)	*dayr felz(en)*

English	German	Pronunciation
roll	das Brötchen (S.Ger.,Aus.) die Semmel, der Weck(en)	dass broetshen dee zemmel, dayr vekk(en)
rolling tobacco	der Shag	dayr shag
roof rack	der Gepäckträger	dayr gepek trayger
room	das Zimmer	dass tsimmer
room number	die Zimmernummer	dee tsimmer noommer
room service	der Zimmerservice	dayr tsimmer zair viss
rope	das Seil	dass zail
rose	die Rose	dee roazer
rosé	rosa	roaza
roundabout	der Kreisverkehr/der Kreisel/	dayr krays fayr kayr/ dayr kraizel/
route	die Route	dee rooter
rowing boat	das Ruderboot	dass rooderboat
rubber	der/das Gummi	dayr/dass goommee
rubbish	der Quatsch	dayr kvatsh
rucksack	der Rucksack	dayr rookzak
rude	unhöflich	oonhoeflikh
ruins	die Ruinen	dee rooeenen
run (cross-country)	die Langlaufloipe	dee lang lowf loyper
run into	treffen	treffen

S

English	German	Pronunciation
sad	traurig	trowrikh
safari	die Safari	dee zafaree
safe	sicher	zikher
safe	das Safe	dass sayf
safety pin	die Sicherheitsnadel	dee zikher haits nardel
sail	segeln	zaygeln
sailing boat	das Segelboot	dass zaygelboat
salad	der Salat	dayr zalart
salad oil	das Salatöl	dass zalartoel
salami	die Salami	dee zalarmee
sale	der Ausverkauf	dayr owsferkowf
salt	das Salz	dass zalts
same	der-/die-/dasselbe	dayr-/dee-/dasszelber
sandy beach	der Sandstrand	dayr zantshtrant
sanitary pad	die Damenbinde	dee darmen binder
sardines	die Sardinen	dee zardeenen
satisfied	zufrieden	tsoofreeden
Saturday	der Samstag/der Sonnabend	dayr zamstark/ zonnarbent
sauce	die Sosse	dee zoaser
sauna	die Sauna	dee zowner
sausage	die Wurst	dee voorst
savoury	herzhaft	hayrts haft
say	sagen	zargen
scarf	der Schal	dayr sharl
scenic walk	der Wanderweg	dayr vandervayk
school	die Schule	dee shooler
scissors	die Schere	dee sheerer
scooter	der Motorroller	dayr moator roller
scorpion	der Skorpion	dayr skorpeeyoan
Scotland	Schottland	shottlant
Scotsman	der Schotte	dayr shotter

English	German	Pronunciation
Scotswoman	die Schottin	dee shottin
Scottish	schottish	shottish
scrambled eggs	das Rührei	dass ruehrai
screw	die Schraube	dee shrowber
screwdriver	der Schraubenzieher	shrowben tseeher
sculpture	die Bildhauerei	dee bilt hower rai
sea	die See/das Meer	dee zay/dass meer
seasick	seekrank	zaykrank
seat	der Platz	dayr plats
seat	der Sitzplatz	dayr zitsplats
seat belt	der Gurt	dayr goort
seat reservation	die Platzkarte	dee platskarter
second	die Sekunde	dee zekoonder
second	zweite	tsvaiter
second-hand	gebraucht	gebrowkht
sedative	das Beruhigungs mittel	dass berooee goongz mittel
see (to)	sehen	zayhen
see (to) (view)	sich ansehen/besich tigen	anzayhen/besikh tigen
self-timer	der Selbstauslöser	dayr zelpst ows loezer
send	(ver)schicken	(fair)shikken
sentence	der Satz	dayr zats
September	der September	dayr zeptember
serious	ernst	ayrnst
service	die Bedienung	dee bedeenoong
serviette	die Serviette	dee zairveeyeter
sewing thread	das Nähgarn	dass naygarn
shade	der Schatten	dayr shatten
shallow	flach	flakh
shampoo	das Shampoo	dass shampoo
shark	der Hai	dayr hai
shave	rasieren	razeeren
shaver	der Rasierapparat	dayr razeer apparart
shaving brush	der Rasierpinsel	dayr razeer pinzel
shaving soap	die Rasierseife	dee razeer zaifer
sheet	das Laken	dass larken
sherry	der Sherry	dayr sherry
shirt	das (Ober)hemd	dass (oaber)hemt
shoe	der Schuh	dayr shoo
shoe polish	die Schuhcreme	dee shookraymer
shoe shop	das Schuhgeschäft	dass shoogesheft
shoemaker	der Schuhmacher/ Schuster	dayr shoomakher/ shooster
shoes (mountaineering)	die Bergschuhe	dee bayrk shooer
shop	einkaufen/einholen	ainkowfen/ainhoalen
shop	der Laden	dayr larden
shop assistant	die Verkäuferin	dee fayrkoyferin
shop window	das Schaufenster	dass showfenster
shopping centre	das Einkaufszentrum	dass ainkowfs tsentroom
short	kurz	koorts
short circuit	der Kurzschluss	dayr koorts shlooss
shorts	die kurze Hosen	dee koortser hoazen
shoulder	die Schulter	dee shoolter
show	die Show/die Schau	dee shoa/dee show

shower	die Dusche	*dee doosher*
shutter	der Auslöser	*dayr owsloezer*
side	die Seite	*dee zaiter*
sieve	das Sieb	*dass zeep*
sign	unterschreiben	*oontershraiben*
sign	das Schild	*dass shilt*
signature	die Unterschrift	*dee oonter shrift*
silence	die Stille	*dee shtiller*
silver	das Silber	*dass zilber*
silver-plated	versilbert	*fayrzilbert*
simple	einfach	*ainfakh*
single	unverheiratet/ledig	*oonfayrhai-rartet/laydikh*
single	der Junggeselle/die Junggesellin	*dayr yoong gezeller/ dee yoong gezellin*
single	Einzel-	*aintsel-*
single (ticket)	einfach	*ainfakh*
sir	mein Herr	*main hayr*
sister	die Schwester	*dee shvester*
sit	sitzen	*zitsen*
sit down	sich setzen	*zikh zetsen*
size	die Grösse	*dee groersser*
ski	Ski fahren/laufen	*sheefahren/lowfen*
ski boots	Skischuhe	*sheeshooer*
ski goggles	die Skibrille	*dee sheebriller*
ski instructor	der Skilehrer	*dayr sheelairer*
ski lessons/class	die Skistunde(n)	*dee sheeshtoonder(n)*
ski lift	der Skilift	*dayr sheelift*
ski pants	die Skihose	*dee sheehoazer*
ski pass	der Skipass	*dayr sheepass*
ski slope	die Skipiste	*dee sheepister*
ski stick	der Skistock	*dayr sheeshtok*
ski suit	der Skianzug	*dayr sheeantsook*
ski wax	das Skiwachs	*dass sheevakhs*
skiing (cross-country)	der Langlauf	*dayr langlowf*
skimmed	halbfett	*halpfett*
skin	die Haut	*dee howt*
skirt	der Rock	*dayr rock*
skis	die Skier	*dee sheeyer*
skis (cross-country)	die Laufskier	*dee lowf sheeyer*
sleep	schlafen	*shlarfen*
sleeping car	der Schlafwagen	*dayr shlarfvargen*
sleeping pills	die Schlaftabletten	*dee shlarf tabletten*
slide	das Dia	*dass deear*
slip	der Unterrock	*dayr oonterrock*
slip road	die Auffahrt	*dee owffahrt*
slow	langsam	*langzarm*
slow train	der Nahverkehrszug	*dayr narfayrkairs tsook*
small	klein	*klain*
small change	das Wechselgeld	*dass vekhselgelt*
small change	das Kleingeld	*dass klaingelt*
smell	stinken	*shtinken*
smoke	der Rauch	*dayr rowkh*
smoke	rauchen	*rowkhen*
smoked	geräuchert	*geroykhert*
smoking compartment	das Raucherabteil	*dass rowkher aptail*
snake	die Schlange	*dee shlanger*
snorkel	der Schnorchel	*dayr shnorkhel*

snow (verb)	schneien	*shnaien*
snow	der Schnee	*dayr shnay*
snow chains	die Schneekette	*dee shnayketter*
soap	die Seife	*dee zaifer*
soap box	die Seifenschachtel	*dee zaifen shakhtel*
soap powder	das Seifenpulver	*dass zaifen pullfer*
soccer	der Fussball	*dayr fussball*
soccer match	das Fussballspiel	*dass fussball shpeel*
socket	die Steckdose	*dee shtekdoazer*
socks	die Socken	*dee zokken*
soft drink (lemonade)	die Limonade	*dee limonarder*
soft drink	das Erfrischungs-getränk	*dass ayrfrishoongs getrenk*
sole (fish)	die (See)zunge	*dee (zay)tsoonger*
sole	die Sohle	*dee zoaler*
solicitor	der Rechtsanwalt	*dayr rekhts anvalt*
someone	jemand	*yaymant*
sometimes	manchmal	*manshmarl*
somewhere	irgendwo	*eergentvo*
son	der Sohn	*dayr zoan*
soon	bald	*barlt*
sorbet	das Sorbet	*dass sorbay*
sore	das Geschwür	*dass geshvuer*
sore throat	die Halsschmerzen	*dee halz shmayrtsen*
sorry	Entschuldigung/ Verzeihung	*entshool deegoong/ fayrtsayoong*
sort	die Sorte	*dee zorter*
soup	die Suppe	*dee zoopper*
sour	sauer	*zower*
sour cream	der Sauerrahm	*dayr zowerrarm*
source	die Quelle	*dee kveller*
south	der Süden	*dayr zueden*
souvenir	das Andenken/das Souvenir	*dass andenken/dass zooveneer*
spaghetti	die Spaghetti	*dee shpagetti*
spanner (open-ended)	der Gabelschlüssel	*dayr garbel shluessel*
spanner	der Mutternschlüssel	*dayr muttern shluesell*
spare	die Reserve	*dee rezayrver*
spare parts	die Ersatzteile	*dee erzats tailer*
spare tyre	der Reservereifen	*dayr rezayrver raifen*
spare wheel	das Reserverad	*dass rezayrverrart*
speak	sprechen	*shprekhen*
special	besonders	*bezonderz*
specialist	der Spezialist/ der Facharzt	*dayr shpetseealist/dayr fakhartst*
speciality	die Spezialität	*dee shpetseea lee tayt*
speed limit	die Höchst-geschwindigkeit	*dee hoekhst geshvindikh kait*
spell	buchstabieren	*bookh shtarbee ren*
spicy	gewürzt	*gewuertst*
splinter	der Splitter	*dayr shplitter*
spoon	der Löffel	*dayr loeffel*
sport	der Sport	*dayr shport*
sports (to do)	Sport treiben	*shport traiben*
sports centre	die Sporthalle	*dee shporthaller*
spot	der Platz/Ort	*dayr plats/dayr ort*
sprain	verstauchen	*fayrshtowkhen*

spring	der Frühling	*dayr fruehling*
square	der Platz	*dayr plats*
square	quadratisch	*kvadrartish*
square metre	der/das Quadratmeter	*dayr/dass kvadrart mayter*
squash	das Squash	*dass skvash*
stadium	das Stadion	*dass shtadeeon*
stain	der Fleck	*dayr flek*
stain remover	das Fleckenmittel	*dass flekken mittel*
stairs	die Treppe	*dee trepper*
stalls	das Parkett	*dass parkett*
stamp	die Briefmarke	*dee breefmarker*
start	starten/anlassen	*shtarten/anlassen*
station	der Bahnhof	*dayr barnhoaf*
statue	das Standbild/das Denkmal	*dass shtantbilt/dass denkmarl*
stay (verb)	bleiben	*blaiben*
stay (verb)	wohnen	*voanen*
stay	der Aufenthalt	*dayr owfenthalt*
steal	stehlen	*shtaylen*
steel (stainless)	der (rostfreie) Stahl	*dayr (rosstfraier) shtarl*
stench	der Gestank	*dayr geshtank*
sting	stechen	*shtekhen*
stitch (med)	nähen	*nayhen*
stock	die Brühe	*dee brueher*
stockings	die Strümpfe	*dee shtruempfer*
stomach	der Magen/der Bauch	*dayr margen/dayr bowkh*
stomach ache	die Magenschmerzen/die Bauchschmerzen	*dee margen shmayrtsen/dee bowkh shmayrtsen*
stomach cramps	die Bauchkrämpfe	*dee bowkh krempfer*
stools	der Stuhl(gang)	*dayr shtool(gang)*
stop	halten	*halten*
stop	die Haltestelle	*dee halter shteller*
stopover	die Zwischenlandung	*dee tsvishen landoong*
storm	stürmen	*shtuermen*
storm	der Sturm	*dayr shtoorm*
straight (hair)	glatt(es Haar)	*glatt(ez har)*
straight ahead	geradeaus	*gerarderows*
straw	der Trinkhalm	*dayr trinkhalm*
strawberries	die Erdbeeren	*dee ayrtbeeren*
street	die Strasse	*dee shtrarsser*
street side	die Strassenseite	*dee shtrarssen zaiter*
strike	der Streik	*dayr shtraik*
study	studieren	*shtoodeeren*
subtitled	untertitelt	*oonterteetelt*
succeed	glücken	*gluekken*
sugar	der Zucker	*dayr tsooker*
suit	der Anzug	*dayr antsook*
suitcase	der Koffer	*dayr koffer*
summer	der Sommer	*dayr zommer*
summertime	die Sommerzeit	*dee zommertsait*
sun	die Sonne	*dee zonner*
sun hat	der Sonnenhut	*dayr zonnenhoot*
sunbathe	sich sonnen	*zikh zonnen*
Sunday	der Sonntag	*dayr zonntark*
sunglasses	die Sonnenbrille	*dee zonnenbriller*
sunrise	der Sonnenaufgang	*dayr zonnen owf gang*

Word list

147

sunset	der Sonnenuntergang	*dayr zonnen oonter gang*
sunstroke	der Sonnenstich	*dayr zonnenshtikh*
suntan lotion	die Sonnen(schutz)-creme	*dee zonnen(shoots) kraymer*
suntan oil	das Sonnen(schutz)öl	*dass zonnen(shoots)oel*
supermarket	der Supermarkt	*dayr zooper markt*
surcharge	der Zuschlag	*dayr tsooshlark*
surf	surfen	*zoorfen*
surf board	das Surfbrett	*dass zoorfbrett*
surgery	die Sprechstunde	*dee shprekh shtoonder*
surname	der Nachname	*dayr nakhnarmer*
surprise	die Überraschung	*dee ueber rashoong*
swallow	runterschlucken	*roonter shlooken*
swamp	der Sumpf	*dayr zoompf*
sweat	der Schweiss	*dayr shvaiss*
sweet (a)	das Bonbon	*dass bonbon*
sweet (nice)	lieb	*leep*
sweet (sugary)	süss	*zuess*
sweetcorn	der Mais	*dayr maiss*
sweetener	der Süßstoff	*dayr zuess shtoff*
sweets	Süssigkeiten	*zuessikh kaiten*
swim	schwimmen/baden	*shvimmen/bardern*
swimming pool	das Schwimmbad/(spa)die Badeanstalt	*dass shvimmbart/dee barder anshtalt*
swimming trunks	die Badehose	*dee barder hoazer*
swindle	der Betrug	*dayr betrook*
switch	der Schalter	*dayr shalter*
synagogue	die Synagoge	*dee zuena goager*

T

table	der Tisch	*dayr tish*
table tennis	das Tischtennis	*dass tishtennis*
tablet	die Tablette	*dee tabletter*
take	nehmen	*naymen*
take	dauern (time)	*dowern*
take pictures	fotografieren	*foto grafeeren*
talcum powder	der Talkpuder	*dass talkpooder*
talk	reden	*rayden*
tampons	die Tampons	*dee tampons*
tap	der (Wasser)hahn	*dayr (vasser)harn*
tap water	das Leitungswasser	*dass laitoongs vasser*
taste	probieren	*probeeren*
tax free shop	der Taxfree-Shop	*dayr taksfree-shop*
taxi	das Taxi	*dass tarksi*
taxi stand	der Taxistand	*dayr tarksishtant*
tea	der Tee	*dayr tay*
teapot	die Teekanne	*dee taykanner*
teaspoon	der Teelöffel	*dayr tay loeffell*
telegram	das Telegramm	*dass taylaygramm*
telephone (by)	telefonisch	*taylayfoanish*
telephoto lens	das Teleobjektiv	*dass taylay obyek teef*
television	der Fernseher	*dayr fayrnzayer*
telex	das Telex	*dass teleks*
temperature	die Temperatur	*dee temperatoor*
temporary filling	die Notfüllung	*dee noatfueloong*
tender	zart	*tsart*
tennis	das Tennis	*dass tennis*

tennis ball	der Tennisball	*dayr tennisbarl*
tennis court	der Tennisplatz	*dayr tenhisplats*
tennis racket	der Tennisschläger	*dayr tennis shlayger*
tent	das Zelt	*dass tselt*
tent peg	der (Zelt)hering	*dayr (tselt)hayring*
terrace	die Terrasse	*dee terasser*
terribly	entsetzlich	*entzetslikh*
thank	danken, sich bedanken	*danken, zikh bedanken*
thank you	vielen Dank	*feelen dank*
thanks	vielen Dank	*feelen dank*
thaw	tauen	*towen*
the day after tomorrow	übermorgen	*ueber morgen*
theatre	das Theater	*dass tayarter*
theft	der Diebstahl	*dayr deepshtarl*
there	da/dort	*da/dort*
thermal bath	das Thermalbad	*dass termarlbart*
thermometer	das Thermometer	*dass termomayter*
thick	dick	*dik*
thief	der Dieb	*dayr deep*
thigh	der Oberschenkel	*dayr oaber shenkel*
thin	dünn/mager	*duenn/marger*
things	die Sachen	*dee zakhen*
think	denken	*denken*
third	das Drittel	*dass drittel*
thirst	der Durst	*dayr doorst*
this afternoon	heute nachmittag	*hoyter nakhmittark*
this evening	heute abend	*hoyter arbent*
this morning	heute morgen	*hoyter morgen*
thread	der Faden	*dayr farden*
thread	das Garn	*dass garn*
throat	die Kehle	*dee kayler*
throat lozenges	die Halstabletten	*dee hals tablet ten*
throw up	(sich) erbrechen	*(zikh) ayrbrekhen*
thunderstorm	das Gewitter	*dass gevitter*
Thursday	der Donnerstag	*dayr donnerstark*
ticket (admission)	die (Eintritts)karte	*dee (aintritts)karter*
ticket (travel)	die (Fahr)karte	*dee (far)karter*
ticket	das Ticket	*dass ticket*
tie	die Krawatte	*dee kravatter*
tights	die Strumpfhose	*dee shtroompf hoazer*
time	die Zeit	*dee tsait*
times	mal	*marl*
timetable	der Fahrplan	*dayr farplan*
tin	die Dose/die Büchse	*dee doazer/dee buekhser*
tip	das Trinkgeld	*dass trinkgelt*
tissues	Papiertaschentücher	*papeer tashen tuekher*
toast	das Toastbrot	*dass toastbroat*
tobacco	der Tabak	*dayr tabak*
tobacconist's	der Tabakladen	*dayr tabaklarden*
	(Aus.) die (Tabak) trafik	*dayr tabaklarden* *dee (tabak) trafeek*
toboggan	der Schlitten	*dayr shlitten*
today	heute	*hoyter*
toe	der Zeh/die Zehe	*dayr tsay/dee tsayer*
together	zusammen	*tsoozammen*

toilet	die Toilette	*dee twarletter*
toilet	das W.C.	*dass vaytsay*
toilet paper	das Toilettenpapier	*dass twarletten papeer*
toiletries	die Toilettenartikel	*dee twarletten arteekel*
tomato	die Tomate	*dee tomarter*
tomato purée	das Tomatenmark	*dass tomarten mark*
tomato sauce	der Tomatenketchup	*dayr tomarten ketchup*
tomorrow	morgen	*morgen*
tongue	die Zunge	*dee tsoonger*
tonic water	das Tonic	*dass toanik*
tonight	heute nacht	*hoyter nakht*
too much	zuviel	*tsoofeel*
tool	das Werkzeug	*dass vayrktsoyk*
tooth	der Zahn	*dayr tsarn*
toothache	die Zahnschmerzen	*dee tsarnshmayrtsen*
toothbrush	die Zahnbürste	*dee tsarnbuerster*
toothpaste	die Zahnpasta	*dee tsarnpaster*
toothpick	der Zahnstocher	*dayr tsarnshtokher*
top up	nachfüllen	*nakhfuellen*
total	total/insgesamt	*totarl/insgezamt*
tough	zäh	*tsay*
tour	die Rundreise	*dee roontraizer*
tour guide	der Reiseführer	*dayr raizerfuerer*
tourist card	die Touristenkarte	*dee tooristen karter*
tourist class	die Touristenklasse	*dee tooristen klasser*
Tourist Information Office	das Fremdenverkehrsbüro	*dass fremden fayrkayrz buero*
tourist menu	das Touristenmenü	*dass tooristen menue*
tow	(ab)schleppen	*(ap)shleppen*
tow cable	das (Ab)schleppseil	*dass (ap)shlepzail*
towel	das Handtuch	*dass hanttookh*
tower	der Turm	*dayr toorm*
town	die Stadt	*dee shtatt*
town hall	das Rathaus	*dass rarthowz*
town walk	der Stadtrundgang	*dayr shtatroontgang*
toy	das Spielzeug	*dass shpeeltsoyk*
traffic	der Verkehr	*dayr fayrkayr*
traffic light	die Verkehrsampel	*dee fayrkayrs ampel*
train	der Zug	*dayr tsook*
train ticket	die Fahr-/Bahnkarte	*dee far-/barnkarter*
train timetable	der Fahrplan	*dayr farplarn*
trainers	die Sportschuhe	*dee shportshooer*
translate	übersetzen	*ueber zetsen*
travel	reisen	*raizen*
travel agent	das Reisebüro	*dass raizer buero*
travel guide	der Reiseführer	*dayr raizerfuerer*
traveller	der/die Reisende	*dayr/dee raizender*
traveller's cheque	der Reisescheck	*dayr raizershek*
treacle/syrup	der Sirup	*dayr zeeroop*
treatment	die Behandlung	*dee beshandloong*
triangle	das Dreieck	*dass draiek*
trim	kürzen	*kuertsen*
trip	der Ausflug/die Reise	*dayr owsflook/dee raizer*
trouble	die Beschwerde	*dee beshverder*
trout	die Forelle	*dee foreller*
trunk code	die Vorwahl	*dee forvarl*

Word list

try on	anprobieren	*anprobeeren*
tube (inner)	der Schlauch	*dayr shlowkh*
tube	die Tube	*dee toober*
Tuesday	der Dienstag	*dayr deenstark*
tumble drier	der Trockner	*dayr trokner*
tuna	der Thunfisch	*dayr toonfish*
tunnel	der Tunnel	*dayr toonnel*
turn	das Mal	*dass marl*
TV	das T.V./Fernsehen	*dass tayfow/ fayrnzayhen*
TV guide	die Rundfunk- und Fernsehzeitschrift	*dee roont foonk- oont fayrn zay tsait shrift*
tweezers	die Pinzette	*dee pintsetter*
tyre	der Reifen	*dayr raifen*
tyre lever	der Reifenheber	*dayr raifen hayber*
tyre pressure	die Reifenspannung	*dee raifen shpannoong*

U

ugly	hässlich	*hesslik*
umbrella	der Regenschirm	*dayr raygensheerm*
under	unten	*oonten*
underground	die U-Bahn	*dee oo-barn*
underground railway system	das U-Bahnnetz	*dass oo-barnnets*
underground station	die U-Bahnhaltestelle	*dee oo-barn halter shteller*
underpants	die Unterhose	*dee oonterhoazer*
understand	begreifen	*begraifen*
underwear	die Unterwäsche	*dee oôntervesher*
undress	sich freimachen/(gen.) sich ausziehen	*zikh fraimakhen/ zikh owstseehen*
unemployed	arbeitslos	*arbaitsloas*
uneven	ungleichmässig	*oon glaikh mayssig*
university	die Universität	*dee oonee vayrsee tayt*
unleaded	bleifrei	*blaifrai*
up	nach oben	*nakh oben*
urgency	die Eile	*dee ailer*
urgent	dringend	*dringent*
urine	der Harn	*dayr harn*
usually	meistens	*maistens*

V

vacate	räumen	*roymen*
vaccinate	impfen	*impfen*
vagina	die Vagina	*dee vageena*
vaginal infection	die Scheidenentzünd-ung	*dee shaiden ent tsuen doong*
valid	gültig	*gueltikh*
valley	das Tal	*dass tarl*
valuable	wertvoll	*vayrtfoll*
van	der Lieferwagen	*dayr leefer vargen*
vanilla	die Vanille	*dee vaniller*
vase	die Vase	*dee varzer*
vaseline	die Vaseline	*dee vasseleener*
veal	das Kalbfleisch	*dass kalpflaish*
vegetable soup	die Gemüsesuppe	*dee gemuezer zupper*
vegetables	das Gemüse	*dass gemuezer*

Word list

vegetarian	der Vegetarier	*dayr vegetareeyar*
vein	die Ader	*dee arder*
venereal disease	die Geschlechtskrank-	*dee geshlekhts krank*
	heit	*hait*
via	über	*ueber*
video recorder	der Videorecorder	*dayr video recorder*
video tape	das Videoband	*dass videobant*
view	die Aussicht	*dee owszikht*
village	das Dorf	*dass dorf*
visa	das Visum	*dass veezum*
visit (verb)	besuchen	*bezookhen*
visit	der Besuch	*dayr bezookh*
vitamin	das Vitamin	*dass vitameen*
vitamin tablets	Vitamintabletten	*vitameen tabletten*
volcano	der Vulkan	*dayr voolkarn*
volleyball	der Volleyball	*dayr volleyball*
vomit	sich erbrechen	*zikh erbrekhen*

W

wait	warten	*varten*
waiter	der Ober	*dayr oaber*
waiting room	das Wartezimmer	*dass varter tsimmer*
waitress	die Kellnerin/	*dee kelnerin/*
	die Serviererin	*dee zayrveererin*
wake up	wecken	*vekken*
Wales	Wales	*vaylz*
walk	der Spaziergang	*dayr shpatseer gang*
walk (verb)	spazierengehen	*shpatseeren gayhen*
wallet	die Brieftasche	*dee breeftasher*
wardrobe	der Kleiderschrank	*dayr klaider shrank*
warm	warm	*varm*
warn	warnen	*varnen*
warning	die Warnung	*dee varnoong*
warning triangle	das Warndreieck	*dass varn draieck*
wash	waschen	*vashen*
washing	die Wäsche	*dee vesher*
washing line	die Wäscheleine	*dee vesher lainer*
washing machine	die Waschmaschine	*dee vashmasheener*
washing-powder	das Waschmittel	*dass vashmittel*
wasp	die Wespe	*dee vesper*
water	das Wasser	*dass vasser*
water ski	das Wasserski	*dass vassershee*
waterproof	wasserdicht	*vasserdikht*
wave	die Welle	*dee veller*
wave-pool	das Wellenbad	*dass vellenbart*
way	die Weise	*dee vaizer*
way (path)	der Weg	*dayr vayk*
we	wir	*veer*
weak	schwach	*shvakh*
weather	das Wetter	*dass vetter*
weather forecast	der Wetterbericht	*dayr vetter berikht*
wedding	die Hochzeit	*dee hokhtsait*
Wednesday	der Mittwoch	*dayr mitvokh*
week	die Woche	*dee vokher*
weekend	das Wochenende	*dass vokhen ender*
weekend duty	der Notdienst	*dayr noatdeenst*
weekly ticket	die Wochenkarte	*dee vokhen karter*

welcome	willkommen	*villkommen*
well	gut	*goot*
west	der Westen	*dayr vesten*
wet	nass	*nass*
wetsuit	der Surfanzug	*dayr zoorfantsook*
what	was	*vass*
wheel	das Rad	*dass rart*
wheelchair	der Rollstuhl	*dayr rollshtool*
when	wann	*van*
where	wo	*vo*
which	welch-(-e,-er,-es)	*velkh-(-e,-er,-es)*
whipped cream	die Schlagsahne/	*dee shlarkzarner/*
	der Schlagrahm	*der shlarkrarm*
	(Aus.) das	*dass shlarkoberz*
	Schlagobers	
white	weiss	*vaiss*
who	wer	*vayr*
wholemeal	das Vollkorn	*dass follkorn*
wholemeal bread	das Vollkornbrot	*dass follkornbroat*
why	warum	*vahroom*
widow	die Witwe	*dee vitveh*
widower	der Witwer	*dayr vitver*
wife	die Frau	*dee frow*
wind	der Wind	*dayr vint*
windbreak	der Windschutz	*dayr vintshoots*
windmill	die Windmühle	*dee vint mueler*
window	das Fenster	*dass fenster*
windscreen wiper	der Scheibenwischer	*dayr shaiben visher*
wine	der Wein	*dayr vain*
wine card	die Weinkarte	*dee vainkarter*
winter	der Winter	*dayr vinter*
witness	der Zeuge	*dayr tsoyger*
wonderful	herrlich	*hayrlikh*
wood	das Holz	*dass holts*
wool	die Wolle	*dee voller*
word	das Wort	*dass vort*
work	die Arbeit	*dee arbait*
working day	der Arbeits-/der	*dayr arbaits-/dayr*
	Werktag	*vayrktark*
worn	abgenutzt	*apgenootst*
worried	beunruhigt	*be-oonroo-ikht*
wound	die Wunde	*dee vunder*
wrap (gift)	einpacken	*ainpakken*
wrist	das Handgelenk	*dass hantgelenk*
write	schreiben	*shraiben*
write down	aufschreiben	*owfshraiben*
written	schriftlich	*shriftlikh*
wrong	falsch/verkehrt	*falsh/fayrkayrt*

Y

yacht	die Yacht	*dee yakht*
year	das Jahr	*dass yahr*
yellow	gelb	*gelp*
yes	ja	*yar*
yesterday	gestern	*gestern*

yoghurt	der/(Aus.) das Joghurt	*dayr yoghoort*
you (polite)	Sie	*zee*
you too	gleichfalls	*glaikhfals*
youth hostel	die Jugendherberge	*dee yoogent hayr bayrger*

Z

zebra crossing	der Zebrastreifen	*dayr tsebra shtraifen*
zip	der Reissverschluss	*dayr raiss fayr shlooss*
zoo	der Zoo	*dayr tsoo*

Word list

Basic grammar

1 Nouns

German nouns are divided into three types, known as genders:
masculine, feminine, and neuter. German also has a system of cases
for its nouns, four in number, and referred to in English as Nominative
(for the subject), Accusative (for the object), Genitive (the possessive
case), and Dative (the *to* or *for* case).

2 Definite article (the)

	Masculine	Feminine	Neuter
Nominative	**der**	**die**	**das**
Accusative	**den**	**die**	**das**
Genitive	**des**	**der**	**des**
Dative	**dem**	**der**	**dem**

The plural is the same for all:

Nominative	**die**
Accusative	**die**
Genitive	**der**
Dative	**den**

3 Indefinite article (a or an)

	Masculine	Feminine	Neuter
Nominative	**ein**	**eine**	**ein**
Accusative	**einen**	**eine**	**ein**
Genitive	**eines**	**einer**	**eines**
Dative	**einem**	**einer**	**einem**

Note that when masculine and neuter nouns are in the possessive
(genitive) case, they have an s at the end, not totally unlike English; **der
Hund des Mannes** (the man's dog).

4 Plurals

Nouns can be rather erratic. There are a few basic principles:

Nouns ending in **-keit** and **-heit** and **-ung** add the letters **-en** to form
the plural.

Neuheit (novelties) becomes **Neuheiten** (novelties); **Sehenswürdigkeit**
(something worth seeing, tourist attraction) becomes
Sehenswürdigkeiten (tourist attractions); **Hoffnung** (hope) becomes
Hoffnungen (hopes). Also, as a general rule, if a word ends in an **-e**,
assume you can make the plural by adding an n; **Witwe** (widow)
becomes **Witwen** (widows).

In the case of masculine and neuter nouns making the plural not
infrequently involves making a change in the vowels within the word
as well as adding an ending. Try adding the sound **-e** or **er** to the
singular form, and you should be able to put the meaning across.

In the plural form of the Dative case, all nouns add an **-n**. **Berg**
(mountain) is a masculine noun (**der Berg**), and becomes **Berge** in the
plural (mountains); on the mountains becomes **auf den Bergen**.

5 Adjectives

Adjectives come in front of the noun. There is an arrangement for making the adjective agree with the noun if it is used without any article (no the or a), which is basically like **der, die, das**; Black thing, for example, is **schwarzes Ding**, pretty woman is **schöne Frau**, big dog is "**grosser Hund**".

If we place an article before the adjective, things are easier; the black thing is **das schwarze Ding**, the pretty woman is **die schöne Frau**, the big dog is **der grosse Hund**. Of the black thing; **des schwarzen Dings**. Of the pretty woman; **der schönen Frau**. Of the big dog; **des grossen Hunds**. (You may also hear **Dinges** and **Hundes**.)

6 Adverbs

Adverbs are essentially the same in German as adjectives; in other words, he does it well is **er tut es gut** (*err toot ez goot*), which means he does it good. Know one and you know the other.

7 Pronouns

	First	Second	Third		
	(I)	(you)	(he)	(she)	(it)
Nominative	**ich**	**Sie**	**er**	**sie**	**es**
Accusative	**mich**	**Sie**	**ihn**	**sie**	**es**
Dative	**mir**	**Ihnen**	**ihm**	**ihr**	**ihm**

The forms for the plural, they, are **sie, sie, ihnen**.

Accordingly, he sees me becomes **er sieht mich**; she sees him: **sie sieht ihn**. I see it: **ich sehe es**.

The dative case is the case which occurs mostly if prepositions are involved (with, by, from, for example).

There is also a form for you which is used for close friends, talking to very small children, and animals; this is **Du**, and should be avoided unless you are really sure of your ground. There is a plural form of this, **ihr**.

The usual word for you is **Sie** (pronounced *zee*), and when written always has a capital letter for its forms, to distinguish it from the forms for they.

8 Verbs

German verbs, like English verbs, come in two kinds, traditionally referred to as strong and weak. Weak verbs are the regular ones, and are easy; strong verbs are irregular, and can really only be learnt. An example of a weak verb in English is to walk; I walk, I walked, I have walked. An example of a strong verb is to swim; I swim, I swam, I have swum.

The weak verbs make their forms which indicate action in the past in a regular way, too: I was loving is **ich liebte**; he was loving **er liebte**; we/you/they were loving: **Wir/Sie/sie liebten**. The strong verbs change the vowel in the main part of the verb: **ich schwimme** becomes **ich schwamm** (I swam).

A German weak verb looks like this:

Lieben,	To love
ich liebe	I love (also doubles up for I am loving, I do love)
(Du liebst)	(you love; this is the very friendly form)
er/sie/es liebt	he/she/it loves
wir lieben	we love
Sie lieben	you love
sie lieben	they love

The other difference between weak and strong verbs occurs in the past participle. Weak verbs are regular in their past participles; add the letters **ge-** to the front, and replace the **-en** at the end of the verb by a **-t**. **Lieben** (to love) gives us a past participle **gelebt** (loved); **spielen** (to play) gives **gespielt** (played), and so on.

Strong verbs do not make this change; e.g. **schwimmen** gives us **geschwommen** (**swum**), sehen (to see) gives us **gesehen**.

A quick look at the verbs "to have" and "to be":

Haben	To have
ich habe	I have
(Du hast)	(you have; very friendly form)
er/sie/es hat	he/she/it has
wir/Sie/sie haben	we/you/they have

Sein	To be
ich bin	I am
(Du bist)	(you are; very friendly form)
er/sie/es ist	he/she/it has
wir/Sie/sie sind	we/you/they are

In principle, the past form I have (done something) is created by using the relevant part of **haben** for verbs which have an object (I have seen him: **ich habe ihn gesehen**; I have done it: **ich habe es getan**), and the relevant parts of sein for verbs which do not have an object (I have swum: **ich bin geschwommen**; I have come: **ich bin gekommen**; I have flown: **Ich bin geflogen**). Bear in mind that, in the past form using have, the past participle comes at the end of the sentence.

9 Prepositions

in means in or into
auf means on or onto
mit means with
zu means to
for means for
bei means with or in the vicinity of (but rarely by)
von means of or from

Most prepositions are associated with the dative case, although some are found with the accusative e.g. **in der Stadt** : IN the town, **in die Stadt**: INTO the town.